"Don Mayer's *Letters to Peter* is not only a touching and very engaging book, it is also a magnificent example of effective grief work. Starting out with sorrow and rage he progresses to serious contemplation of the deeper questions of life, death, and healing. He allows the reader to experience this very personal journey of healing. I strongly recommend this book to anyone who has or even hasn't experienced this kind of grief and loss."

—Susan Koch, retired schoolteacher

"Some ministers leave people wondering if they are actually real human beings or just someone playing a role. Though we never doubted the reality of Don's humanity, this volume confirms it's depth, grace, and passion."

—Anthony B. Robinson, author of *Common Grace*

"Don Mayer's eloquent letters to his dead son express many of the conflicting feelings that we share when a beloved person dies: debilitating grief, overwhelming sadness, continuing disbelief, persistent loneliness. But also anger at the absent person, anger at those whose efforts to offer comfort may be clumsy or tactless, anger at God. Gradually, Don's letters reveal a path to acceptance, and even gratitude, through the redemptive power of family, friends, music, prayer, ordinary activities, and faith in the One who has 'been our dwelling place in all generations.'"

—Susan Delanty Jones, retired lawyer and parent who lost a young child

LETTERS TO PETER

LETTERS *to* PETER

~

*On the Journey
from Grief to Wholeness*

Donald E. Mayer

Prologue by Herbert Anderson
Epilogue by Walter Brueggemann

CASCADE *Books* · Eugene, Oregon

LETTERS TO PETER
On the Journey from Grief to Wholeness

Cascade Books
An Imprint of Wipf and Stock Publishers
199 W. 8th Ave., Suite 3
Eugene, OR 97401

www.wipfandstock.com

ISBN 13: 978-1-60899-104-4

Cataloging-in-Publication data:

Mayer, Donald E.
    Letters to Peter : on the journey from grief to wholeness /
Donald E. Mayer, with Prologue by Herb Anderson and Epilogue by
Walter Brueggemann.

    xx + 174 p. ; 23 cm.

    ISBN 13: 978-1-60899-104-4

    1. Grief—Religious aspects. 2. Bereavement. 3. Children—
Death—Psychological aspects. 4. Pastoral theology. I. Anderson,
Herbert, 1936–. II. Brueggemann, Walter. III. Title.

BF575.G7 M43 2010

To Lynnea, Linda, and Chelsey,
With love, admiration and gratitude,
And for Tim and Sue, Sarah and Jim
And the cousins: Miles and Erin,
Hannah and Peter.

And thanks to 'first editor'
Ulrike Guthrie!

I looked, and a scroll was stretched out before me . . . and written on it were words of lamentation and mourning and woe. And he said to me, 'eat this scroll.' . . . Then I ate it; and in my mouth it was sweet as honey.

(Ezekiel 2:9—3:3)

Contents

Preface

In the spring of 1998 our son Peter was killed in an auto accident, plunging his wife, Linda, their five-year-old daughter, Chelsey, and all of our family into relentless, painful grief. This book is an account of that grief—and of what helped us to move though the "shadow of death" into fullness of life once more. In my career as a pastor I am accustomed to responding to similar events in others' lives. It is usually in writing, often in a sermon for a memorial service. Thus it is not surprising that I wrote a piece for the memorial service for Peter.

What is different about that memorial piece is that it was not addressed to the people gathered for the memorial. It was addressed to Peter. And it was the first of a series of letters I felt compelled to write to Peter expressing my grievous, pain-filled response to his death.

Except for the letter read at Peter's memorial service, each letter was addressed exclusively to Peter. At first, I shared the letters only with my wife, Lynnea, and our widowed daughter-in-law, Linda. Now I offer these letters to you. While each situation of loss is unique, you may find much in these letters that resonates with your own experience. It would not be true to say that everyone belongs to a company of believers. But it is true that at some time all of us belong to a company of grievers.

In the first section of the book the letters are in effect a day-by-day journal of the grief of a mom and dad for a deceased son. In the second section of the book, I explore what helped us to grieve well, probing the mys-

tery of how comfort and fullness of life do come to us—
in spite of the neverending loss of our son.

Tears and anger, doubt and fear, pain and "if-onlys"
are all present here, as they no doubt also are in your
particular grief. But you will also see here the attention
of caring friends, and a repeated decision to trust in a
God who pays attention to us and cares.

Years ago in a long dark winter I was often sustained by the hope that my painful experience might
someday be helpful to someone else. Now in that hope I
offer to you these letters to Peter.

Prologue

HERBERT ANDERSON

This collection of letters from a father to his son after the son's tragic and untimely death is a bold invitation to reconsider grief in several significant ways.

The experience of absence and the feeling of emptiness are common in grief. The loss of someone we love leaves a hole in the soul that can never be filled. "It would be nonsense," Dietrich Bonheoffer once wrote, "to say that God fills the gap; God doesn't fill it, but on the contrary, keeps it empty and so helps us to keep alive our former communion with each other, even at the cost of pain."[1] In the absence of someone we love, we tell stories of his or her past presence in our lives. The pain of this remembering includes an increased awareness of absence, the permanent "never-to-be-ness" of death. Eventually, as the grief diminishes, one becomes more accustomed to the presence of absence.

Lament for a Son by Nicholas Wolterstorff is another account of a father's grief over a son's untimely death as a result of a mountain-climbing accident at age twenty-five.[2] The book is testimony to a remarkable young man whose love of the mountains and hiking in solitude led to his death. There is no effort to relieve the sadness that accompanies remembering a young life cut off before a future filled with promise can unfold. As a

1. Dietrich Bonheoffer, *Letters & Papers from Prison* (New York: Touchstone, 1997) 176.

2. Nicholas Wolterstorff, *Lament for a Son* (Grand Rapids: Eerdmans, 1987).

father, Wolterstorff is baffled and hurt by his son's tragic death and overwhelmed by the pain of absence.

The letters in this book presume an absent presence in which the invisible boundary between the living and the dead is permeable. Don Mayer, the father, often prefaces some activity report to his dead son Peter with phrases like "as you have seen" or "as you may know." This awareness that his dead son lives close enough to see what is happening changes the emphasis of grief from absence only to *absent presence*. These letters were difficult for Don to write because they kept alive a relationship that will never again be what it was. "Your absence is an awful black hole which keeps sucking at your presence in our lives, so that we must keep talking about you, and holding to each other." On one occasion, when Don had borrowed his son Peter's shoes, the father imagines his dead son saying with a laugh, "Hey, Dad, need a little help tying my shoes?" The vividness of Peter's presence in death is a continuation of the vitality and exuberance of his living. And the intimacy of these letters pulsates with the affection of a father for his son.

The death of a child is against nature. It is profoundly wrong for a child to die before his or her parent. It is difficult enough to bury our parents but our parents belong to the past. Our children belong to our future. When a child dies, something of our future dies. Over and over again, Don shakes his head in disbelief. "Six weeks ago at this time you were already dead and we didn't know it. And I still don't believe it." Disbelief is about the struggle to internalize an unimaginable reality. Sometimes the father's disbelief comes from the struggle to hold the joy of his life alongside the deep sadness of his son's death. It is also the suddenness that fosters disbelief. "When everything was going so well for you, for the whole family, suddenly you are out of it. Forever." When Don admits that he does not want to understand why his son is absent, disbelief turns to denial.

Prologue

Grief happens without our intending it when we lose someone we love. We are often overwhelmed by waves of sadness or choked by tears that flow freely and unpredictably. *But grief is also something we discover.* The work of grieving is the intentional search for memories and meaning that accompany loss. "That is the reason I write to you," Don Mayer confesses to Peter, "to find out what it is like to lose a son the way we lost you." One of the gifts of remembering is the discovery of new stories of the deceased person or additional dimensions of his or her person. After hearing stories from friends and colleagues of Peter, Don Mayer writes this to his son: "It had simply not occurred to me just how much you lived a kind of calling which you may never have verbalized—a calling as a Christian businessman." There were other surprises that were more difficult but the end of the remembering was a picture of a real person with remarkable gifts.

How people die affects how we grieve. Grief is certainly shaped by the nature and intensity of our relationship to the lost person or object. In recent years, however, we have learned to pay attention to the uniqueness of grief after violent death. Remembering has particular pain and particular importance when the death is violent. Three weeks after Peter's death, his father wondered how he died. "One sleepless night I did have this image of your head encrusted with dried blood. I wanted to wash it away, cleanse the wound, hold your head." Ted Rynearson, a psychiatrist who lives on the same island as Don and Lynnea Mayer, has written about "restorative retelling" of an individual's living in order to find release from compulsive retelling of the dying.[3] These letters to Peter witness to the healing and transformative power of telling and retelling and retelling again.

3. Edward K. Rynearson, *Retelling Violent Death* (Philadelphia: Brunner-Routledge, 2001).

The honest expression of anger toward his son is one of the prohibitions about grief that Don Mayer violates in these letters. This taboo has its origins in the cultural belief that the living dead (spirits of the departed) actively influence daily living. If the dead are actively involved in our living, one should not offend these spirits by speaking ill of them. The anger may be old—a residue of a conflicted relationship that preceded the death. Sandra's mother had sabotaged every romance that Sandra had. Sandra stopped grieving for her mother's death when she was invited to consider her rage at her mother for messing with her life. When anger that is part of grief cannot be expressed, all grief may be buried to keep the anger hidden.

Sometimes the anger is more recent and related to how someone died. Less than a week after his son Alexander was killed in a car accident in a terrible storm, William Sloan Coffin preached these words at Riverside Church. "Do you think it was the will of God that Alex never fixed that lousy windshield wiper of his, that he was probably driving too fast in such a storm, that he probably had had a couple of frosties too many? Do you think it is God's will that there are no street lights along that stretch of road, and no guard rail separating the road and Boston Harbor?"[4] It should never be said when someone dies that it is the *will of God.* The younger brother of Alex said it accurately in front of the casket: *You blew it, buddy. You blew it.* Do not blame God for human carelessness.

Coffin's sermon is a prelude to these vividly painful letters from Don Mayer to his son Peter. Both died much too young because they were careless about drinking and driving. It was not the will of God. There is no

4. William Sloane Coffin, Jr. "Alex's Death." A sermon preached at Riverside Church in New York City, January 21, 1983. In *The Collected Sermons of William Sloane Coffin*, Vol. 2, *The Riverside Years (Years 1983–1987)* (Louisville: Westminster John Knox, 2008) 3–5.

reason to be angry at God. There is reason, however, to be angry at Alex and Peter for how they died. The anger about Peter's death is most vivid when Peter's parents and his widow read the death certificate: "contributing cause of death: acute ethanol intoxication." What a stupid way to die, the father laments. "I hate the way your drunk death twists our grief." What is most remarkable about these letters by Don Mayer is that a father's anger does not become a "bottomless pit" but the way to recover his intense love for his son. Anger will not bring Peter back but neither does it sever the bond between a father and his son.

The anger toward Peter does not last forever. The police report indicated skid marks on the road suggesting that he had not fallen asleep. Something else happened. Peter's friends insisted that there was no sign when he left the party that he would have any trouble making the five-minute drive to where he lived. "So we are left again with sudden accidental death. And not knowing. And not blaming. Anybody. Not you either, Peter." From that moment on, the anger toward Peter is mostly gone. What is left is simply grief.

One of the tasks for a family when a significant member dies is to acknowledge the loss of both the person and his or her role in the family and then redefine family roles accordingly. Whenever Peter's brother and sister gather with his parents, it always seems to Don that part of the family is missing. What is missing in particular is Peter's role as the "multiplier" in the family. "What we miss is not simply your presence, but what your presence created among us—all the interactions that you produced among us." The family is quieter when it gathers without Peter. Sometimes families quickly elect someone to assume that role as a way to avoid the loss. Although Peter's family did not seek to replace his "multiplier" role, his daughter grew to mirror her father in that respect.

Peter's sister had the most difficult time grieving his death. She had given birth to her second child just a month before Peter's death. It is difficult to live simultaneously with the joy of new life and sadness of life lost. To complicate matters, the child was named Peter.

Less than three months after Peter's death, Don and his wife, Lynnea, celebrated her wedding anniversary with Peter's widow, Linda. "We clinked glasses and toasted Linda's 10th Anniversary of becoming part of our family." Linda was now first of all a member of the family rather than Peter's wife. "No more wedding anniversaries," she said. Roles and family rituals had already been redefined.

There are a number of common truths about uncommon grief that we are invited to discover in these letters from a grieving father to his dead son.

- Grieving people feel transparent, as if the whole world can see a soul in sadness. As Don Mayer opens his billfold to pay for the wine, the flight attendant says "Forget it!" waving him off with a secretive smile. "How could she know?" he asked Peter. The painful paradox for grievers is that they want their grief heard without the messiness of being seen as grievers.

- It is tempting to varnish the story of a life or a death to fit our preconceived hopes or dreams. "The consensus in the family is that you swerved to miss one of the abundant deer in that neighborhood—but who knows?" The family was free to grieve fully when they determined to tell the truth about the role of alcohol in Peter's tragic death.

- We often use negative images to describe the process of grieving. We will say someone "broke down" or "fell apart" when their grief was expressed in sobs and tears or in erratic and uncharacteristic behavior. Don Mayer has it just right. "Falling apart now and then (actually pretty often) is part of what will eventually put us back together." It is often our fear of not being put back together again that keeps us from the "falling" that makes healing in grief possible.

- The end of intense grieving is a second loss. Don Mayer was aware of that change when he stopped writing to Peter for some time. People need to hold on to their grief because it may be the only thing they have left of someone they loved and lost. People are sometimes reluctant to share their grief with others out of fear that they would take the grief away or invalidate the sadness.

- Our culture discourages men from grieving. They must be strong and tearless. Tears are a sign of weakness and only women are permitted to be weak. While Don Mayer did not set out to write a countercultural account of a man grieving, his frequent references to sobbing uncontrollably or being held by his wife as he cried and cried present an alternative to male stoicism in the face of devastating loss. These letters also reveal a human struggle to maintain the thin veneer between the intense internal pain grievers feel and the façade the world expects from them. Don was able to write these letters because he was held by people who did not expect him to hide his sadness.

- Grievers often find it difficult to embrace moments of joy in their lives in the midst of sadness. The years following Peter's death were filled with incredible abundance and joy. Perhaps because it does not seem right to have such rich life experiences while Peter is dead, Don did not write to his son for five years. Eventually Don writes that "your loss no longer shadows the glad times in the way that it did." "I want to share with you the deep joy of this time, these times, this year marked not so much by your death but by celebrations of fifty years of marriage." When sadness no longer cancels the joys of living, grievers know that the darkest part of the journey is over.

These letters chronicle a journey that parallels the biblical psalms of lament. Walter Brueggemann, whose epilogue concludes this collection of letters, had convinced Don Mayer that it was "very much ok to pour out my anger to God." In these letters, the anger is more directed toward Peter than God but for similar reasons: abandonment and absence. Eventually, in the biblical psalms, angry complaints about God's absence are replaced by quiet confidence in God's enduring presence. Peter is gone, the hole his death left in his father's life is still there, but the memory of this beloved son is constant and sweet. These letters chronicle that journey from sadness to sweetness. They are also compelling testimony to the necessity of taking that journey. Healing from grief is found where our wounds hurt most. We discover those wounds through persistent remembering and storytelling. Sometimes it becomes necessary to "write my way out of grief," as Don did.

I have known Don and Lynnea since shortly after Peter's death. The authenticity of their lives is reflected on these pages. So is the affection for them from people they have loved. The people that sustained them with love and hugs and accepting presence were people who had earlier received love from Don and Lynnea. I did not know Peter, but knowing Don I understand about the "multiplier effect" that he attributes to Peter. The same might be said for Don and Lynnea. While these letters have been written largely from a father's perspective, their willingness to face the sadness together made it possible for each of them to live through their own unique grief. Their confidence in the promise of God's understanding made it possible to take that grief journey, not knowing what they would discover on the way. I end with these words from Don that bear witness to the kind of faith that makes grieving possible. *"Our own trust in God's understanding and acceptance of our feelings gave your mom and I the permission to express without hesitation all the pain, shock, anger, all the 'if only's, the emptiness, brokenness and sadness which we felt in the aftermath of your death, all the tears, the whimpering, the earth-shaking sobs: you got it all in these letters, Peter, week after week, month after month. And so did God. We trust that God understood and accepted all that."*

PART 1

Through the Dark Valley

Before Our World Was Shattered:
Two E-Mails from Pete

November 21, 1997
Dad—

Yesterday I got a call from my friend in Birmingham. He has a pretty good job opening that he would like me to come and check out. (This would be a pay increase of about $45,000 per year—an unbelievable thought to me). He would like Linda and I to come on 12/5. I am going to talk with him on this Saturday a.m. for more precise info.

Can you and Mom come down to stay with Chelsey that weekend?

By the way, are you coming down over Thanksgiving? Would you be staying here then?

I think I told you that I stopped in to see grand-father. You are very correct—he does seem to be declining rapidly. I am not sure that he knew my name. Pretty sad . . .

Pete

November 22, 1997 (in response to an e-mail from me)
Hi Dad—

Boy, a lot of thinking to do.

I think of the huge salary increase as a rainy day thing and as offering the possibility for early retirement—at least early retirement from the HAVE TO WORK ALL THE TIME standpoint. And also, "Gee, it would be nice to have Chelsey in college comfortably without a big mortgage," so that if I want to work part time I can do that.

Tenure is a big question. But one thing I can negotiate is stock options. If we get bought the stock price increases fairly substantially. So I can get one of the "golden parachute" type of deals. I fully expect that to occur in 4 to 7 years.

Then there's the matter of getting back to the NW. That is my biggest fear—having a tough time moving back. I really enjoy our proximity to the mountains, the coast, Bend, etc., and we have close friendships here. And it is tough to leave a good job that is going well.

And the toughest part of all is moving away from the family network. Even though we may go a month between visits, it is really tough to leave Tim and Sarah, and you and mom so far away. And Chelsey loves her cousins.

If we go, the bank would purchase our home and pay for moving, so there are no costs to the move.

The best part of the job we are thinking about is that it is a great senior level position in a company that is 10 times my bank's current size—plus the perfect job. If I could choose a job, this would be it.

So it is a lot to think about.

I don't know yet when we will go for the interview, but I will talk with you as soon as I know. Thanks for the thoughts and prayers.

Pete

From the Order of Service for Peter Karl Mayer, April 11, 1998

Hillsdale Community United Church of Christ, Portland, Oregon

Peter Karl Mayer was born to Donald and Lynnea Mayer on May 15, 1960, in Mexico, Missouri. He attended elementary school and three years of high school in St. Louis, where he played percussion with his brother Tim, pianist, in the high school jazz band. He graduated from high school and from Northern Illinois University in Dekalb, Illinois where he led the University Marching Drummers.

Beginning in high school, Peter worked for the First National Bank in Dekalb until moving to Portland, Oregon, in 1985, to continue his career in banking. Peter's brother Tim, and Tim's wife, Susan, had already moved to Portland. His sister Sarah followed after graduating from Iowa State University.

With their three offspring in Portland, Don and Lynnea answered a call to Eagle Harbor Church, Bainbridge Island, Washington, joining their children in the Northwest.

Peter met Linda Lacey while she and Peter worked in the same building. They were married April 30, 1988, at First Congregational United Church of Christ in Portland, with Peter's father presiding. Their daughter, Chelsey, was born January 9, 1993.

While working consecutively with the Oregon Bank, the Bank of America, and Pacific One Bank, Peter with Linda was involved with many volunteer services. Peter served on the Board of Habitat for Humanity in Portland.

At the time of his death, Peter was beginning a new position as Senior Vice President with the Compass Bank in Birmingham, Alabama.

Boating, skiing, volleyball, golf, and fine woodworking projects were among Pete's many enthusiasms. Above all, Peter was enthusiastic about people and life.

Peter was killed in a one-car accident Sunday evening, April 5, in Birmingham, at the age of thirty-seven.

Peter's brother Tim played three pieces during the service: Summertime, St. Louis Blues, and Margaritaville. His sister, Sarah Skutt, read three scriptures: Psalm 23, Isaiah 61:1–4, and Romans 8:31–39. The Reverend Jim Halfaker, a long-time friend and colleague of Don and Lynnea, presided at the service, and read this letter from Don addressed to Peter.

Dear Peter,

I am writing this on Wednesday afternoon, April 8, as a draft for something which might be read at your Memorial Service. I do not want to be doing this. I have always liked writing about you. I've had nearly forty years of writing for memorial services and I'm good at it. But, as Jim Halfaker said to me a couple of days ago, "Its just for the wrong person, isn't it."

He's right: fine memorial service but for the wrong person.

Tim gave us the news, you know. I fumbled for the phone in the dark bedroom, snorting about middle of the night wrong numbers, but then Tim got right to it, with wordsounds forever chiseled deep into my soul: ". . . very, very bad news. Peter was killed tonight . . ."

When we stopped for gas about 3 a.m. on the way from Bainbridge Island to your place in Portland, I doubled over with the convulsive sobs which go on and on whenever the reality of your death penetrates my protective denial. Your Mom held me with I suppose the same comforting tenderness with which she held you when you were little and frightened. My vocalized sobs were saying, "I don't want, I don't want, I don't want . . ."

The little child in me as well as the mature adult does not want your death, Peter.

Dammit Peter, why didn't you wear that seat belt?!

You know, of course, that ever since the news got around we've had practically a continuous party at your house. It is odd to call it a party because whenever somebody arrives we are convulsed with sobs all over again. But then we start talking about you, and pretty soon, we are convulsed with laughter. Same stomach muscles involved, I've noticed. And we are going to party again right after this service and again for you and Linda's 10th anniversary and again for your 38th B.D. I am telling you this because I know how much you love parties and you are going to miss all this. Serves you right. But we've got to party because you are missing, and we need to throw all the bright resources we can martial against the dark powers of death to which your death has left us so vulnerable.

Earlier today, mom and I saw your body. It was the first time we'd seen your body since that wonderful family weekend you arranged for us at Sun River. My favorite image of your body from that weekend is of you and Chelsey coming down the slope at Mt. Bachelor, you holding your ski pole out as a tow bar for Chelsey. It never entered my mind that I would ever see your body when you were not in it. Your body looks pretty good, considering. Mom remarked that you had become more bald than we had previously noticed. I thought you looked a little older. But it was unquestionably your body because it had your particular smile, that smile you always had when you knew something. Naturally, there are all kinds of opinions going around about why you are smiling, some of which are crude, rude, and even lewd. But as soon as I got back to your house I knew why you were smiling: there was your brother Tim, shirt off, sweating profusely, worn out with mowing *your* lawn.

Until then, of course, given my clergy background, I had a more theological reason for your smile.

For example, I could imagine you saying, "Dad, you remember how often you pointed out that some people criticized Jesus for being such a party-giver? And that time when the wine ran out at the wedding party and Jesus changed the bath water into the best wine ever? Well, Dad, wait till you see what a party Jesus throws here for us newcomers!"

From my Christian faith perspective, I am assuming that you are aware of all that is going on with us, Peter. I figure I'd best make all the use of the faith that I can. So I suspend all my disbelief, and assume that you are present with all of us with your characteristic warm, gentle, robust love. But dammit, Peter, you are such an absent presence.

You absence is an awful black hole which keeps sucking at your presence in our lives, so that we must keep talking about you, and holding to each other.

I never realized before this week how much you and Tim and Sarah are virtual Siamese triplets joined hip and shoulder, and now you are torn out of the middle. Dammit Peter, we had three children, and we loved it that way. And you and Linda having become one, and Chelsey—God, Peter, what gaping emptiness you've left all over the place.

So in your absence, we keep telling stories about your presence. Mom was just remembering the time in St. Louis, that Sunday morning, when I was already at church, and as usual Mom was going through the hectic work of getting you three out the door and you saw the cat about to escape and you helpfully slammed the door, unfortunately not quite quickly enough to avoid nearly amputating his tail. And I got this frantic phone call from Mom describing our bloody Siamese cat orbiting our living room at somewhere near the ceiling level and could I manage to come home and do something about it?

And I remember that weekend in the Ozarks, when you were about 12, just around this time of the year, the warm night air perfumed with spring, frogs croaking down at the creek, campfire glowing near our tent, and I will never forget the way you said, "Wow, Dad, this is really neat!" smiling with surprised delight at how unimaginably good the time was. It is like the smile which your body is wearing now, Peter, perhaps because you have once again discovered an unimaginably good time.

I've said it thousands of times, but this time I'm asking it for us: "Now to the One who by his power at work among us is able to do far more than we ever dare to ask, or even imagine . . ." We are daring to ask God for all the love God can pour out for us. We need it. And we need each other so much. Of course, we believe that you are okay now. But we worry about the rest of us— because we loved you so much. You loved us greatly too, in ways which were only yours Peter. There was no love like it ever before nor will there ever be another love like it, because nobody else will ever be you among us.

Fortunately, we believe that God knows what it feels like for us to lose you, God knows how much we disbelieve that we can get through it all without you. We trust that God understands how it is with us. God went through his own holy week once and surely God hurts for our hurt. But after the horror of good Fridays, and the black emptiness of those Saturdays, there are Easter Sundays. We trust that in time, with the comfort of God's compassionate, life-giving spirit, we will come to know about Easter more fully than ever before.

We trust you already know about Easter, Peter, more fully, personally, and wonderfully than you had ever imagined. And maybe that is another reason for your smile.

Unbelievable Absence

Dear Peter,

As I write the words "Dear Peter" I find myself shaking my head. I discover myself doing that a lot, while I'm sitting, walking, and driving, quite without being aware of it at the time. I suppose that means that I still can't believe that you are gone, forever, irrevocably out of our lives, and that you have been out, gone, for eleven days. I can't take it in. I suppose I shake my head because I don't want to take it in.

When we drove away from the church Saturday morning, having brought pictures of you and the stone oil lamp and the candle, I saw the hearse bringing your body up Capitol Highway. It was quite a jolt. Later, I thought your body looked less like you than it did when Mom and I saw it on Wednesday. But it certainly looked enough like you to set Chelsey and all the rest of us into long, heavy, wailing sobs.

Today, it seems unreal all over again. Less real than last week. Perhaps that's why the sobs which convulse me have not happened for a while. This is now more of a shadowed time, a time when we experience everything from the shadow of your death.

But not all the time, Pete. Sometimes we just seem to forget that your death has happened. The world goes on doing its daily stuff and we go on doing it with the world which does not seem to know that the world has been irrevocably changed. Better to say, the world ended just after ll p.m., April 5 and a new world began so quickly that a lot of the world never noticed. But there are some in that world who notice. A letter came today addressed to "the estate of Peter Mayer."

All of us wish the change were revocable, that the world had not ended. It was a much happier world with you in it, Pete. How often in our fantasies we wish you had had your seatbelt buckled and airbag deployed, allowing you miraculously to escape death.

Chelsey's wish is expressed differently: "Isn't God strong enough to bring my daddy back to life?" It's a question which is far more significant and logical for the season than questions about the Easter bunny. God brought Jesus back, why not Daddy?

The shadow of your death, Peter, falls on everything and often we are angry about it. Sarah sheds tears of rage about the now shadowed joy in the birth of little Peter, because you are not here to hold your namesake.

And what a party we planned to have at Sarah and Jim's new house, celebrating the new place for them plus your move to your new home in Birmingham. You know, not one of us wanted you to go in the first place, but you converted us all with your excitement about it. We will still celebrate at Sarah and Jim's new place but it will be a shadowed celebration.

We all went with Tim and Sue on Easter Sunday afternoon to see the new bed and bath addition to their house. Tim expressed the mood for all of us: "Now we really feel the anger—all the parties are over." Right. And we are left with your deadness, Peter.

Having said that, it was an unbelievable party after your memorial service. You really missed a good one, Pete! It was wonderful for Mom and me to meet and talk with a multitude of your friends. People came down from Bainbridge Island. And two of your best friends from your high school days traveled way across the country—how wonderful to see Kathy and Lisa again!

You must have been a great encourager, Peter. We keep hearing personal testimonies about that. "I'd never be doing such and such if Pete had not got me going with it." We love it that you were so loved. Because you had a love affair going with the world, there is no sting in your death, no venom. That's not to say we are not angry about you leaving us the way you did. There is a sting in your abrupt forever gone-ness.

Since the big party, it's been getting more and more quiet. Few visits, calls. People leaving one by one. I don't feel it so much now as at some other times, but God, I already miss you Peter. Even if I can't believe you are forever gone.

Love, Dad

Auto Reliquary

April 16, later in the day

Dear Peter,

The auto insurance agent in Birmingham called this morning. Paperwork is slow there because they are loaded with claims from the tornadoes. But they will send your stuff back, and the police report. With pictures, I think he said.

He said you had a lot of stuff in your car. Golf clubs, etc. It's odd: it did not occur to me that you would have a lot of stuff with you in the car that they would send back. It's like your stuff survived but you didn't.

As I said before, Pete, each of us at different times gets pretty steamed about your carelessness. We sometimes felt anyway that you didn't pay enough attention to family stuff.

As Tim said you'd go out of your way to help any family person or friend in need—as long as we were up on your screen. But if we dropped off . . . (I think he was remembering the time you were supposed to pick up Miles for the weekend and completely forgot.) So sometimes we thought your peripheral vision was a little limited. We would have loved to have had you and Linda along on Maui last spring. But you'd just changed jobs, and geez, you needed to make your own decisions. Nobody else was in your shoes. But along with all your caring and enthusiasm for people, we wish you could have realized how critical your self-care, self-protection was for all that—so you would have habitually, unthinkingly always fastened your seatbelt. As it is, Linda above all feels cheated out of the future. Helluva deal.

And yet when we saw your body on Saturday Mom and I noticed your smile had faded. I am thinking more and more that you too are grieving for having left us, and feeling guilty about your carelessness—if indeed it was a matter of carelessness, we really don't know.

I had this vivid image of you the other night, looking so sad.

So we imagine you too being held, hugged, patted, and comforted, Peter, encouraged just as you were such an encourager to everybody.

God shall wipe away all tears. Yours and ours.

Love, Dad

Comforting the Impoverished

April 16, still later

Dear Peter,
Jesus talks about the poor man who after a hard life on earth is comforted in the bosom of Abraham in heaven. You were certainly not having a hard life, Pete. But there can be no greater poverty than yours now, Peter, having lost seemingly forever all family and friends.

Our incredulity about your death has almost been matched by an unbelievable outpouring of comforting love and prayers. I suppose we are now experiencing what Jesus said would be true: the strange unworldly blessedness of those who grieve: a seemingly limitless compassion, a tenderness which seeks to tend to our wounds, a kindness (something like I remember Linda speaking of your kindness so unique in her experience,) a gentleness which patiently continues to soothe and heal.

We love you so much, Peter. We trust that such comforting is for you as well.
Love, Dad

Becoming Acquainted with Deadness

Tuesday, April 21

Dear Peter,

I find myself thinking a lot about your deadness. I guess I have never experienced dead before, at least not like you are dead. I find your sudden deadness prompts expletives from me like "crazy," "stupid," "God, so dumb." One moment you were alive, the next you were dead. Thud. Dead. Bonk. Dead. Like swatting a mosquito. Whine. Slap. Dead. A click of a switch. Light. Dark. Alive. Dead. Crack of a limb. Shatter of glass. There. Gone. Like the snap of a seat belt. Alive. Dead. And none of us were there. We weren't even close. We didn't even know. Nobody knew. Alive. Snap. Dead. Just like that.

It is so sudden, Peter, so final, that today I can't take it in. I hardly feel it at all today.

That is one reason I am writing to you. I am trying to reach down into the elusive reality of your death. It is so hard to catch and hold the permanent presence of your forever absence from us.

You've been out of our house anyway for twelve or fifteen years. For ten years you've been with Linda. So your absence for me is an absence of your potential presence, your anticipated presence, vacations, visits, email, phone, promised times, assumed times, dreamed of times, times imagined, fantasized. On screen. Delete. Like the picture frame Mom borrowed for the memorial display to hold that candid shot of you when you were about 11—you were in it and now it's empty again.

But today, forgive me Peter, I don't feel so much saddened as bewildered, a head shaking don't get it, can't get it.

Love, Dad

Shadowed

Tuesday, April 21, later

Dear Pete,

I assume you know that we did gather at Jim and Sarah's new house Sunday night. Susan, Tim, Miles and Erin, and Linda and Chelsey. The kids had a ball exploring the new territory. We did celebrate my birthday, but it was a shadowed celebration. We all knew we had expected it to be combined B.D., new house, and farewell celebration for you and Linda. We probably would have had some tears about that anticipated absence from Portland, an absence which would have had you wonderfully present in Birmingham, however.

Instead Linda reported she had found an apartment in Lake Oswego, indoor and outdoor pools for Chelsey, great bike riding areas. We rejoiced. And as you know, we cried. Too much, Pete: an apartment for two instead of a spacious new home for three.

Monday we went to the zoo. Mom and I, Linda and Chelsey, Sarah, Hannah, and Peter. We bought grandparent passes. We expect we will be here more often. They are good for all the kids, and at other zoos too. Guess which one tops the list? You got it—Birmingham. Damn.

It was a beautiful day, warmest so far this year. At lunch, Hannah and Chelsey ran barefoot in that expanse of green grass in front of the stage. They were a beautiful sight—did you see them? Splendid as it was, Mom and I held Linda and told her how deeply we'd rather have been at the airport saying good-bye to the three of you, with the beauty of your flying-off day supporting our hope, our appeal for the three of you someday returning to the Northwest.

Linda and Chelsey came out to Sarah and Jim's for dinner, bringing a ham that one of the comforters had brought. Again it was good to be together. We want so much now to be together. But it was a shadowed time. The always present shadow of your absence, Peter. Love, Dad

Sudden Accidental Death

April 21, Tuesday, still later

Dear Peter,

Linda showed us a beautiful letter she received from
one of the persons who worked for you those two brief
months in Birmingham. It contributed to my growing appreciation of your work, Peter. I always knew
you did well; I didn't have much understanding of why.
Apparently in addition to your business wisdom, you
were a very warm, loving human being to the persons
with whom you worked. "Pete was interested in us as
persons, not just workers," the letter said.

It occurs to me that you must have been the very
opposite of my stereotyped image of a bottom-line-driv-
en corporate exec. I have always believed that in the corporate world, justice and human concern could never be
adequately legislated, but are finally dependent upon the
grace of God, and the character—I would say Christian
character—of people in policy-making and person-relat-
ing positions. It had simply not occurred to me just how
much you lived a kind of calling which you may never
have verbalized—a calling as a Christian businessman.

I hesitate to use the term "Christian" because for
the last couple of decades it has come to be associated
with attitudes which are narrow, bigoted, judgmental,
and distrustful of the world. You certainly were the opposite of that. Okay, Pete, I promise I will continue to try
to reclaim the term for persons such as yourself.

Well, Peter, the report of your accident should be
arriving today or tomorrow. I hope it comes before I
take off to my meeting in Cleveland. I want to see the
photos, and read what the police said about your sudden
accidental death. I suspect that deep in me somewhere
there is a large lively mass of grief which needs to be ex-

pressed. More sobs to come, I think. Some laughs too, I hope. And, I am sure, lots of close tender moments with Chelsey and Linda, and Mom. And your siblings. And, I guess, close to you too, Pete.

Seeing evidence of your last moments may help me once again to touch and hold for a while the permanent reality of your crazy, instant, deadness.

Alive. Snap. Dead.

Love, Dad

Lots of Memos, but Never Again Close

Thursday, April 23, in flight, Portland to Seattle

Dear Peter,
So here I am on an AirWest express flying through
the rain from Portland to Seattle. From there I'll catch
the flight to Cleveland for the meeting of the United
Church Board for Homeland Ministries. Of course I had
planned to begin the flight in Seattle. But we've still been
in Portland dealing with the aftermath of your death.
This little extra leg is one of a million things we never
expected to be doing, Pete. Because we never expected
you to be dead.

It's raining and we just climbed above a cloud layer.
Once upon a century this would have been the realm
where we would have expected to encounter you. Our
picture of the cosmos is not so simple now. So where are
you, Peter?

You have been dead now for eighteen days. For
the first time this morning I counted the days. Only
eighteen. My God it seems like months. Except often
it doesn't seem at all like you could possibly be dead
already. Yesterday was my 66th birthday, as you know.
Often in years past, I recognized that when they hit their
seventh decade, our friends begin to die more frequently. I don't need to tell you, Pete, that I never expected
you would be dead before me.

My birthday celebration was shadowed as is everything else. The little ones—Hannah, Miles, and usually
Chelsey—escape the shadow. Miles had wrapped a present for me, announcing with proud anticipation as he
offered it, "It's a joke, Grandpa!" It was. After two years
of my laying teasing claim to it, he presented me with
his blanket. When he saw how funny that was for everybody, he immediately took the box back and presented

one at a time another half dozen presents, each of which fit his new category of "joke."

Hannah also presented me with a gift: a card with a noble photo of a bald eagle and a caption reading, "With the recipient's capacity for vision, fortitude, and character, who needs hair?" Well said, right Pete?

I recalled and then Sarah remembered the joke of our Indian Guide names. Remember, you were Flying Eagle and I, naturally, was Bald Eagle. We made a drum, remember, Pete? Out of a wooden nail keg covered with inner tube rubber on top, with a neat eagle painted on the side. We were both pretty proud of it.

Sarah and Jim gave me a couple of Segovia CDs, because they had played one the other night and we enjoyed it so much. And Mom remembered how we'd once heard Segovia in concert at the University of Missouri while Mom was expecting you.

That's the way it is, Pete. Reminders of you all over the place. Even National Public Radio last Saturday featured a guy from Todd, NC, talking about Bone Sucking Sauce, the great stuff we brought you from that old general store. You loved it and we loved the way you loved it.

This morning is one of those times when I am really sad. Missing you. Saddened that the promise of your life with us was so abruptly canceled.

I seem to be more sad about you when I am alone. Two rows in front of me are three guys in business suits talking enthusiastically about some venture in fifty million dollar increments. It is so easy for me to see the trio become a quartet with your presence. From the back, one of the guys even looks like you. But from the front, you'll be glad to know that I think you were a lot better looking. I probably would never have said that out loud to you when you were alive, unless I would have qualified it by saying I'd forgotten to clean my glasses.

Geez Pete, when I think of never seeing your face again—Damn!

I wish I could have observed you in your working world. As we get more and more testimony about your way of working, I see more clearly how delighted people were to find a person such as yourself at a senior v-p. level. And I understand why they wanted you at that level. Maybe Mom and I will yet make a pilgrimage to Birmingham sometime before the memory of you there fades. One of the women who wrote of you so warmly also reported that you knew exactly how many days you had been away from Linda and Chelsey and how many days it would be before you went back to Portland and brought them to Birmingham. As you probably know, you only had fifteen days to go when you hit the tree. God, so close. And now, never again close.

Love, Dad

All Sad

Dear Peter,

Fred, the human resources guy from Compass Bank,
was so proud to report that he had recruited you twice,
once for Bank of America, and again for Compass Bank.
He explained how he had told people in Birmingham
that you were really happy in Portland with your work,
family, and the Northwest and that they would really
need to up the ante to get you away. So, as Tim says, they
kept throwing more money at you. In light of what happened, Fred has no idea how much he sounds like the
serpent in the Garden, or the boa in The Jungle Book:
"Trussssssssst me," and "you will not die."

But the Garden tells of the inescapable risks of being fully human. And there were risks you and I talked
about, Pete, in this opportunity for you to be more fully
you. We just never thought about your habitual risk in
not buckling your seatbelt, dammit. There is still a lot
of anger here, Peter, about you not buckling down for
your family responsibilities—like Sarah's tear-filled rage
because your death has shadowed the joy of little Peter's
birth.

The other night, in the middle of the night when
visualizations of you are particularly vivid, you looked
so sad. A kind of guilty sadness, I thought. God, Peter,
we may be really pissed at you for not using the seatbelt,
but you know we love you, Pete. We did and we still do.
You know we forgive you. We don't want you to be sad.
It hurts again to think of you as sad, just like I suppose it
hurts you now to see us so sad. God must be sad for all
of us.

Talk with you later, Pete.
Love, Dad

Love Letters from Dad

April 23, SeaTac Airport

Dear Peter,

As you can see (can't you?) my breakfast croissant has cooled because I have been writing, so absorbed am I in the process of crafting words to deal with this multi-multi-faceted reality of your deadness, Pete. It is apparent that in the times when I am alone with your absence, I'd rather write to you than eat. But this sandwich cost five bucks and its getting cold!

So why do I want so much to write? All day long and in bed too, I am always thinking of what I want to write to you. Perhaps filling this yellow tablet with my not long legible scrawl is a careful or cautious way of releasing some of the frightening pressure from my grief-filled heart. I know God heals the broken hearted but I resist the breaking.

It's like I used to say about bread in communion: "Notice how the bread resists the breaking."

Perhaps my writing to you is my way of taking control of my grieving, escaping the breaking, avoiding the awe-filled power of those deep sobs. I know that the tears and the wailing are good for us. I just don't want the pain that produces them.

Forgive me, Pete, forgive us for the ways we try to escape your death. We love you so, and we still do not want your irrevocable, unending, never again with us, absence.

Love, Dad

Window Pain

April 23, in flight

Dear Peter,
The tears are here. I'm trying to hide them. I'm sitting next to a young mom with an eight-month-old boy. Cute. Both mom and boy. Warm exchange of information. "I have five grandchildren." "Yes, all in Portland." "Yes, how good they are all nearby."

She didn't ask and I didn't say how many children I have living in Portland. And I try to avoid revealing the thought of how much l ache to have had four grandchildren in Portland plus one just moved to Birmingham.

And the tears just started to flow. They slid down my cheeks like the occasional raindrop slides down the windowpane eight inches away. I turned toward it so that the young mom next to me will not see and will not ask and I will not need to explain. Explain pain. Pane. My Kleenex is wet, frayed, balled. Bawled.

I don't want her to see me and ask for the story. For a young mom, your death is a horror story, a too easily imagined impossible possibility. I don't want her to think about it. So I hide. I'll hide for a while in theology, huh Pete, that long proven useful means of avoiding life. Okay, I am getting a little sarcastic.

There is nothing quite so powerful as your death, Peter, to force us to face our theology.

Take Linda for example. The other night, as you may have noticed, she said she was angry at God. "Of all people, why Peter?" she complains. I deeply appreciate her complaint, but I'm not afflicted with that question. I guess I noticed long ago that there are no exemptions granted good hearts like you, Pete, to the general laws of gravity and motion, and the damage likely to occur to any head caught between an irresistible force and an immovable object. I think you must have unwittingly assumed an exemption based on your thriving, hearty, lusty, raucous love for God's gift of life. When Linda or anybody else asks, "Why Peter?" I say, because you didn't buckle your seat belt.

Yes, I know I've often pointed out to others that about half the psalms are complaints to God about God's mismanagement of fairness issues. I love the passionate, candid anger of those complaints. A long time ago when I heard Walt Brueggemann talk about Ps. 35, my anger-stress induced hemorrhoids disappeared. Right, Pete, so much for the healing power of the Word!

But with your death, I am so convinced that God grieves with us that complaint is not in me. Except toward you—and that too is fading, Peter, as I feel you are grieving as well. We love you Pete. We grieve with you as well as for you.

Love, Dad

God Does Not Take

April 23, in flight, later

Dear Peter,
I'm still taking refuge in theology. Fortunately only a couple of people have suggested that God "took" you, Pete. I hope nobody uses that kind of profanity around Chelsey.

Of course I know people who say such things mean to be kind. But what blasphemy. God as kidnapper. For what? To take you hostage in order to teach us a lesson, demand a submissive faith, only then to renege on the contract to give you back?

Yes, I can see death as God's servant. Years ago James Weldon Johnson's preacher poet spoke eloquently of that. When the suffering is too much, God calls Servant Death.

But that's different from the notion of God taking you for some divinely foreseen, inscrutable purpose. This is not to say, thank God, that God does not invite us to find some life-giving values in your death. Fred is not the only one, for example, who is now committed to buckling his seatbelt. I am sure there will be many more much more profound redemptive values in your manner of death—although a life saved from your fate would certainly be a wonderful redemption.

God does not will everything that happens. But I trust that in everything which happens God works with us for life-saving good. Yet for all the redemptive good we may find from your death, I would rather have you alive, Pete.

There is such burden-lifting helpfulness in those opening lines of our United Church of Christ Statement of Faith: "God calls the worlds into being." God calls, invites, evokes, and creation says "yes" most of the time. But as toddlers, you and Tim and Sarah too illustrated

28

the truth Hosea had noticed: "When Israel was a child, I loved him. Out of Egypt I called my son. The more I called them the more they went from me."

So God is like a good parent—like you were to Chelsey, Pete. God calls, cajoles, encourages, warns, affirms—but does not coerce. Sarah said it so well the other night: "God does not intervene; God invites. Invites all drivers to wear seatbelts, especially husbands and fathers."

God knows we say no to God a lot. Remember that Jacques Barosin portrait of Jesus Mom gave me, which I always had hanging in my office? A picture of Jesus with tears in his eyes, looking out over the city of Jerusalem. When I get home, I'll look at it again.

Love, Dad

Recalling Then, Recognizing Now

April 23, later, in flight

Dear Peter,
I am still on the plane. The captain just pointed out
Glacier Park off to our left.

Remember that trip? You and Tim playing around
the portable bear trap cage in back of our campsite? And
remember how on the way there, in some campground
in Wyoming, you characteristically made friends with
a couple camping in a big powerboat they were towing
to Lake MacDonald? And sure enough, thanks to you
we spent a marvelous day on their boat, with each of
you kids taking a turn at the wheel. It was such a great
time that after about six beers, the boat owner and I
each finally confessed to our occupations: me, clergy, he
labor-union organizer. Neither of us had wanted the ste-
reotypes of those jobs to spoil the day. Maybe your love
of power boating came from that time, Pete.

In terms of making friends with strangers, Chelsey
is so like you it is uncanny. Or canny, depending on
how much stock one invests in genetic predisposition.
Yesterday, for example, when Linda was showing us the
indoor pool at Oswego Pointe (to which she and Chelsey
will be moving), Chelsey strolled over to a guy in a
Jacuzzi at the other end of the pool: "Hi, I'm Chelsey.
What's your name?" She then conversed about the temperature of the water, etc.

It's exactly that kind of winsome friendliness which
you exhibited from the time you could talk. Drove your
elder brother crazy. Remember the time you got to Aunt
Flo's welcoming hug before Tim did, and he bit you?
Remarkably clear entomology of "back-bite."

You probably got that outgoingness from Mom,
who developed it early as an abandoned toddler's survival strategy. Now with Chelsey, Linda and the rest

of us are trying to figure out how to teach Chelsey to approach strangers with some seat-belt restraint, so to speak, without throwing a chill on her warm exuberance.

Ooops. Mom and little son just broke for the john. I'd better go too since I'm in the window seat. Talk with you later.

Love, Dad

Cup Spills Over

Dear Peter,

It's after the potty break and lunch. (Do you know all this before I write it? Do you become aware of this when, only when, I think about it? Where are you, Pete? Are you? Are you you?)

Anyway, two things happened to keep the all-devouring grief-wolf from my door. First—your ex–flight attendant sister will love this—I got blocked in the john. Sarah probably knows that on a 737 when the cabin is tilted upward, it is possible for the door of one rear lavatory when opened to stay open which then prevents the adjacent lavatory door from opening more than about three inches. I now know this too, firsthand. Because that's what happened to me, although it took a while for me to figure out what was blocking my door.

So what does the passenger do once one has accomplished one's purpose in entering the lavatory, and then can't get more than a hand out? Wave? Obviously I need more than a handout!

I could peek out at the passengers. But I was not quite sure I wanted them to peek back.

I pushed the call button a couple of times. Nice bell tone, like I've heard before, which I always thought was some kind of coded communication between cockpit and cabin crew, like "bong, bong" = "breakout parachutes"; "bong" = "just kidding."

The flight attendants were up the aisle serving lunch and didn't seem to notice the bongs, so I was up the creek without a paddle.

Fortunately, in the providence of God, another mom and her youngster came to use the other john and when they closed their door—you got it!—"when God closes one door" (all together now) "another door is opened."

Speaking of the providence of God—how's that for a segue, Peter?—let me tell you about lunch. As if you don't already know. Here's how it went.

The cart is coming. I'm not too hungry. My stomach is queasy because of today's early hour and my stomach's everyday proximity to that cold, deep, volatile pool of grief. Red wine may help. When, thanks to Sarah, Mom and I got bumped up to first class, we always ordered wine with meals. But I am too frugal to pay for it in coach.

I take out my billfold and count my cash. I can probably break for the four bucks.

"Anything to drink with your lunch?"

"Red wine, please," opening my billfold.

"Forget it," she whispers, waving me off with a secretive smile.

And now I'm looking out the window again, hiding my tear-filled eyes, marveling at the providence of God through the kindness of strangers. How could she know?

In the presence of the ultimate enemy, a generous table is prepared for me, cup spilling over—because of the 8-month-old bouncing next to me! But only a dribble overflowed.

Never mind. This cup is God's love poured out for you, for me, in keeping with that strange good fortune, that blessedness of those who grieve. God, Peter, I need it, all the poured out comfort I can get.

Good thing I picked up some extra Kleenex while I was blocked in the john.

Love, Dad

Settling For Easter

April 23 still in flight

Dear Peter,

So what shall we say to this, if God is for us? How often I've used that line from Paul when opening a funeral service. In the face of your hearty life and abrupt death, Pete, what shall we say about the providence of God? God's *provide*-ence, I like to call it. I would say right off the bat that a seatbelt was provided, Peter, but I hate to keep rubbing it in. I think God's providence is like that aforementioned genetic predisposition. There is both gift and risk in Chelsey's exuberant relational initiatives. So we who love her will seek to encourage and nurture and educate and protect. But ultimately she will make her own decisions.

Since Mom and I loved music, we assumed that you three would be genetically predisposed accordingly, and provided the lessons and the instruments. You each chose how to respond to that providence. And we respected your decisions.

So God, the cosmic parent of all of us, who knows us better than we know ourselves, invites, encourages, calls, the resource persons who form the caring network, the nurturing conspiracy, the life-protecting assemblage, for each of us, and according to the kind of persons we happen to be.

Look at it this way, Pete. All of us have been struck by the fact that for everybody in the family, the spring of '98 was going exceptionally well. I think I have never known such a time of uninterrupted happiness in my second career as a (retired) minister-at-large. The scope of friendships, new homes, new grandchildren—never a more wonderful time until Sunday night, April 5.

I know that some might look upon your death in the midst of all our good fortune as fortune's brutal dirty trick—a way of slapping us down, a way to say, see, you had no right to be so happy. And it does feel, has felt, like we were conned, double-crossed, ambushed, cheated.

But there is the other side of it that has me wondering about God's providence. Did God somehow, knowing your predisposition, get each of us involved in all this future stuff, so that we would be pushed, jostled, pulled along, rushed, dragged, however reluctantly into a future without you, but with joy in it nevertheless?

Even your brief future with the Compass Bank gave Linda and Chelsey a financial base from which to move forward. And certainly, thank God, for the compelling concern for Chelsey's future, pulling us forward. Providence.

In some vast, immensely complex, creative, multifaceted, unimaginably subtle ways, did God, knowing the danger in your life-loving exuberance—did God call, suggest, invite, an integrated network of comforters to prepare for us, care for us, provide for us?

How else to explain the inexplicable multitude coincidental acts of comfort, contributing to the priceless blessedness of we who grieve your death? People I have cared little about have cared greatly for me, for us, a most gracious surprise—as well as a gentle judgment upon my harsh judgments.

And such comfort often happens without the comforter having the faintest idea of what she or he is doing. Just a simple act of kindness, like a small bottle of red wine freely offered.

Yet it is you we love Peter, you we want in our lives. For all the providence, for all God's power to work with us for good in spite of your death, for all the cloud of witnesses whose prayers are constantly working to save our lives, in spite of our trust in God's power to do more than we dare to ask or imagine, we'd rather you were down in Birmingham, Alabama, than wherever you are now, just as I have no doubt, Easter lilies notwithstanding, that God and the disciples would rather have had Jesus die in old age still teaching and raising hell with temple and empire.

But we have to go with what we get. You get a Good Friday, you gotta settle for an Easter. Right, Pete?
Love, Dad

The Flight Not Taken

April 23, Detroit airport, on the tarmac, in delayed flight

Dear Peter,

As you may have noticed, just before we were to
roll away from the jetport, a mechanic on the last
walkaround noticed jet fuel leaking. We sat on the
ground for ninety minutes before they canceled the
flight. I napped some of the time. Tried to read. Inane
Jeopardy! on the video. So now I'm sitting where I can
keep an eye on Gate 11, where we are promised another
flight to Cleveland will depart.

These are some moments of alone sadness again. A
guy standing in front of me combing his hair is wearing
a T-shirt that reads "Birmingham" across the back. Easy
to visualize you. The P.A. system just announced a flight
leaving for Birmingham, Gate 1. I walked down for exer-
cise, tearing with the thought of how excited Mom and I
would lave been on hearing that announcement with us
ready to board. Because, thanks to Mom's conservative
financial diligence we just got a big fat tax refund. We
could have spent more flying. Damn.

I'm tired of theologizing. I'm tired of this flight. I'm
just sad about you, Pete.

Love, Dad

P.S. Had you noticed the fuel leak, Pete? Did you somehow bring it to someone's attention? The delay was in-
convenient. Lack of delay may have been fatal. One sudden accidental death in the family is more than enough.

No Sharks in Lake Shasta

April 23—finally, about to depart

Dear Peter,

I want to tell you about a neat little conversation with Chelsey. It happened a couple days after your memorial service. Maybe you overheard it.

"Grandpa, is my daddy still in that box?"

"No, Chelsey, we just used it for the service."

"What did they do with it?"

"Well, Chelsey, they did something called cremating, which means they turned your daddy's body into ashes. Then one of these days we'll go get the ashes and we will put some of the ashes in special places where we want to remember your daddy, like up on Mt. Hood. Uncle Tim is going to put some ashes where he is going to plant a beautiful tree by his new deck. We are going to take some ashes to Bainbridge Island, and we are going to plant a tree in our yard there too. And I am sure you'll put some in Lake Shasta."

"Oh, what about the sharks?"

"Well, there are no sharks in Lake Shasta, Chells, and besides, they wouldn't be interested anyway in ashes."

"I want to put some at our house."

"Sure, Chelsey, that will be fine."

One other day, she came downstairs early just as I was bringing in your paper. Nobody else was up or at least not visible.

"Grandpa, could you just sit down and hold me for a while?"

I did.

We'll all do our best, Pete.
Love, Dad

Bi-Focal Times

April 27—after the meeting, departure from Cleveland

Dear Peter,

As you may know, it is a bright, clear morning, and
I am just about to depart on a flight which will get
me into Portland four hours sooner than my original
schedule. Great! And there are three other UCBHM
[United Church Board for Homeland Ministries] board
members on the same flight, so we had fun hanging out,
waiting, lamenting the lack of Starbucks in the Midwest,
planning a hymnsing on the plane, etc.

Right now in my bright mood, your death seems
like it happened to some other dad on some other planet. I even talked about it with the guys, describing briefly
why I was flying to Portland rather than Seattle, why you
were killed in Birmingham, etc. And what we think happened on that awful Palm Sunday. The consensus in the
family is that you swerved to miss one of the abundant
deer in that neighborhood—but who knows?

I hesitate to tell people about your death. I find I
try to protect them from the need to respond to the horror of the story, and the fact that I am telling it about my
own son.

People say they cannot imagine what it is like to
lose a son the way we have lost you. I can't either. That
is one reason I write to you—to try to find out what it
is like. One thing it is like is that almost every experience has a double perspective. There is the event itself
and at the same time there is the event we see from the
perspective of your death. It is like this morning. I notice
it is a bright spring day. And then I note it is a bright
spring day and you are dead.

Often the two are connected by means of a memory. Like when all of us UCBHM people gathered on
the street in front of the new United Church of Christ

Radisson Hotel and Church Home for the groundbreaking ceremony. Naturally, I thought of how much I would enjoy telling you of the proximity of our UCC national headquarters, not only to the Cleveland Indians' ballpark and the Arena, but also to the Diamondback Brew Pub next door.

I remembered our last phone conversation the week before you were killed. You bragged about an 82-degree day in Birmingham. I countered with the fact that I had eight brands of microbrew in the garage refrig. We lamented the lack of such riches in Birmingham, since "life is too short to drink cheap beer."

It was a lot shorter than we thought.

Doris Powelll, UCC national treasurer, greeted me enthusiastically, and we stood alongside each other. Doris, you know, is one of those beautiful surprises that sometimes happen to us clergy. She was moved by my ministry to her own ordained ministry long after we had left Hope Church in St. Louis, and without my ever knowing it—till we rediscovered each other at FaithWorks, that marvelous national gathering of UCC folk at Purdue University ten years ago. She picked up a degree in accounting before deciding on seminary—when the position of treasurer opened, she was a slam-dunk.

Doris was confirmed at Hope Church when you were a little kid. She remembered you and your siblings. She hadn't heard. A long hug. Tears. I appreciated it.

Some of us worshiped at Sugar Creek UCC on Sunday. The pews were filled, and there were kids of all ages all over the place. Right in front of me was a first grader bouncing all over the pew, scooting off to the bathroom and back again, happily reaching across his dad to sock his sister with her doll just before prayer time. In the coffee time, I told his parents how much he reminded me of my middle son, without saying my "late" middle son.

I wish I were coming home to tell you face-to-face, Pete.

Love, Dad

Comfort in the Extended Family

April 27, In flight from Cleveland

Dear Peter,

If Mom and I were to be separated during this emotional aftermath of your death, it's very good that she could be with your siblings and Linda and their families while I could be with our United Church of Christ family. I have always thought of the UCC that way, having been born into one of the parent denominations, and having grown up as our denomination was beginning. Now, of course, I am more aware of this faith family extending beyond time and space, while enjoying its company right now.

And how comforting the church family has been. Tom Dipko, UCBHM Executive Secretary, acknowledged our loss of you in the opening worship. Many of the people at 700 Prospect Avenue already knew of your death. Nearly everybody I met treated me with a kind of shy gentleness—as though the word had gone out, "he is fragile, handle with care."

Most of the time I was so turned on by engaging conversations, authentic hearty worship, and involvement in significant issues of justice and compassion, that your death seemed like an event which had happened on a planet not of our solar system.

Worlds collided, however, during that special showing of the movie *Amistad*. The film was too busy portraying a silly stereotype of the Congregational Church to bother indicating that the UCBHM originated out of Congregational support for Amistad ex-slaves. But that's the reason all two hundred of us saw it.

I must say, Pete, that the scene where the ex-slaves win the first trial and the young attorney leaps, shouts, and flips—it so very easy to visualize what I heard of your response to your first birdie just a few hours before you were killed.

42

And in one of the more moving moments of the film, I discovered how thin and porous the membrane separating my ordinary deep feeling responses from that vast, volatile pool of grief I carry around. My eyes filled with tears. My stomach tightened. I looked at the ceiling and the floor and saw you both places. I just wanted to go someplace and sob, Pete.

I thought about doing just that when the film ended. Our UCC President and General Minister, Paul Sherry, had urged me to call him whenever I wanted to talk about your death. I thought about calling him to ask if I could just come over and cry. But then some of the church family engaged me, and they gently carried me away from one of those convulsive encounters with the reality of your death.

Some time later, I told one of the Church Home staff about what happened to me in the film. She hastened to assure me, as did others, that it would have been okay to have left and cried. I explained that I was seated in the middle of the row, and *Amistad* was an assignment that I wanted to complete.

But my headache came again, Pete. The pain centered between my eyes, the pain that comes from crying too long, or from trying too long not to cry.

Love, Dad

No Rewind

Dear Peter,
As I said to Sarah last night on the phone, while I cherish my larger UCC family here, I have missed in these days the presence of some really close, longtime friend. Erv Bode came closest to filling that role, even though we have hardly seen each other since Elmhurst College. We share a common church heritage. His wife's dad and your grandfather Mayer were best friends at Elmhurst College and Eden Seminary. Erv and Jo have three adult children too, all doing well just as you three were all doing well.

Erv and I sat in the lounge of the conference hotel and talked a long time. On the way back to the room, I asked Erv to wait a moment while I went to get him a copy of your memorial bulletin and my first letter to you. I don't know yet when it's okay to do that. So far I've only given a copy to Tom Dipko. I want everybody to see it, but at the same time I feel like I'm using it to draw inordinate attention to myself. I am also aware that I wrote the letter only three days into trying to deal with your death. I don't know how it will read to somebody else, or how it will read to me six months or six years from now.

But the long conversation with Erv somehow made it okay to ask him if he'd like to have it. I think it was one particular comment from Erv which made it okay.

I had described how you died—that it had been such a wonderful day for you, as well as for Mom and me a couple thousand miles away—up until the moment you hit the tree, seatbelt not buckled. Erv said, "It seems so unnecessary."

Geez, Pete. That sure says it. It is a feeling that I, we, come back to again and again.

We keep wanting to rewind the videotape, play it over, have it come out differently. My head tells me not to mess with the "if onlys," but my heart goes there again and again. Simple insignificant neglect with such enormous life-and-death significance. Click. Life. No click. Death.

God, how could it be, how can it be that we, I, you, all of us should suffer such an irreparable tearing, so quickly, so finally, with no time to warn or to protest or to fight for life even against impossible odds, no time to pray, to hang on to even impossible hope.

Instead, dead. Just like the period at the end of this sentence. Dead. Period. Unnecessary. Dead. O Peter, I don't want, I don't want, I don't want, I don't want—
Love, Dad

Tearing the Bread

April 27, in flight later—

Dear Peter,

I'm sorry l left you with that awful centering on the unnecessary-ness of your death. Surely if you are as alive and aware as my faith claims you must be, surely you must be grieving even more than we the missed moment when you might have simply lifted your left hand to grab the metal insert and click it into the buckle.

Surely if we are comforted so, I trust you too must be lovingly comforted by the God who wipes away all tears. And by all the company in heaven.

That phrase—all the company in heaven—is used in our communion service. It was used last night. I never expected you to be among that company in heaven. My mom, yes. We will be glad when my dad joins them, with I'm sure a triumphant welcome for the old young and fearless prophet. But you, Pete? What the hell are you doing there?

Psalm 90 did not fit my present take on God's relation to the inhabitants of the universe. Thou shalt not dash thy head against the car door frame. Thou shalt not smash thyself into a tree.

And John 15? Greater love has no one than the one who lays down his life for his friends. Yes, dammit, that is the way it is supposed to be, so that grief may be mingled with some honor and gratitude. But you didn't lay it down—you simply did not protect it. My God.

I was close enough to the table to see that the loaf was pre-cut almost all the way through. Bad symbolism. Pretense. Denial. Don't avoid the work of the breaking, and the observing, noticing the particular way each particular loaf resists the breaking. Notice the tearing, the scattered crumbs, the messiness.

46

The wine was poured, rich dark red, good to see. I noticed for the first time that it really even looks like spurting blood. Did you bleed much, Peter? We don't know yet. Maybe we never will. One sleepless night I did have this image of your head encrusted with dried blood. I wanted to wash it away, cleanse the wound, hold your head.

"Poured out for you." Yes, for a long time I've believed that Jesus accepted execution willing to trust that somehow thereby people who loved him might come to see that nothing, not even his death and their cooperation in it, could separate them from God's love. So we, I, hang on to that, Pete, trusting that somehow God is hanging on to you and to us.

Your communion and my communion with all the company in heaven was just too much not to cry about, Peter. You may have noticed the tears streaming down my cheeks during most of that service.

You cried like that at my mom's memorial service, more than anyone else I think. Do you still cry now, Pete? Are spiritual bodies equipped with tear ducts?

"God will wipe away all tears." Everybody's. Individually. Tenderly. Personally. I hope so. Yours, ours, mine.

Love, Dad

Biologically Precious

Dear Peter,

I'm very glad I was able to get a flight that will take me
into Portland a whole four hours earlier than my original schedule. Of course in my really original schedule,
I'd have been in and out of Seattle. But now with you
dead, I want to see the rest of the family. It's more than
mere want. I have what seems to be a patriarchal bio-
logical need to see and hear and touch each one. God,
how can Linda stand the daily absence of your presence?
At least for the rest of us, your presence was not daily.
Somehow since your death happened, I have begun to
see each one of my offspring differently, seeing each
of you with more fullness, more individuality, more
strength. Linda, Tim, Susan, Sarah, Jim, Mom. You too,
Peter. Your persons are now more precious.

Love, Dad

The Most Absorbing Story

4/27 Still in flight to Portland

Dear Peter,

In that conversation the other night Erv asked if I was having any trouble concentrating. I said, "Not often."

That's true. I think there was a genetic element in your tendency toward intense focus to the neglect of other legitimate claims for your attention. I am usually engaged with people and not distracted even by the constant interplay between what is happening and what is happening from the perspective of your deadness. And I read theological stuff with no problem, probably because all good theology is multibiographical and in reading it becomes autobiographical. Which means I am dealing with you, Pete, even when I am reading theology.

But I don't read a novel very well. I've got a good one, and I've read it some. But nothing at this point is as absorbing as the story of your death and our and my reaction to it.

So I constantly want to write rather than read.

I hope you are alive and getting these, Pete.

Love, Dad

P.S. I just had this image of you saying to me in some kind of time and place, "Wow, Dad! I really appreciated all those letters!"

Immeasurable Evidence, Address Unknown

4/27 Still later in flight—

Dear Peter,
The fact is I don't have your present address. It is not so much a question of to be our not to be, as "Is you is or is you ain't?"

Like everybody else in our particular faith family, I am a child of the Enlightenment. Scientific method and all that. Experimental results replicated. If it's not measurable, it is not real.

Once you were measurable, Pete. We have photographic evidence. You are now immeasurable. And we are experiencing immeasurable grief. There is no doubt about the living reality of our grief, however immeasurable. So how about the living reality of you, Pete, even though you are now immeasurable?

The Pilgrim Press display at UCBHM featured a book called *The Humanizing Brain.* Apparently a very erudite investigation of the physiological validation of our religious sensitivities. I think it might offer the chance of some measurable possibility of the survival of some of your brain power, Peter, that part of you which makes you essentially you. But I'd already put too many books on my REI credit card. So I postponed the purchase. I suppose there will never be enough facts to offset the fact that I do not have an address for these letters to you.

Faith, like love, is ultimately a decision. But for me, it helps when my faith decisions are supported by some cosmological construct. Some microphysical, macro-physical, quantum-physical theorem to support my metaphysic. And so am encouraged by every new scientific discovery which messes up all the old scientific beliefs in an essentially materialistic, soon to be measured, dead universe. I delight—and did even before you were killed, Pete—in every hint that the universe is after all essentially organic, alive, immeasurable, above all relational, and in its ultimate expression, personal.

I do not believe that the essence of all being is meaningless. It makes absolutely no sense to me to reject as sentimental the notion that the self-giving love of God is the living heart of the cosmos. My assaulted and defiant heart says, "Yes! In the beginning was the meaning through which all is created, and the meaning lived among us, and enabled us to see ourselves as children of the meaning."

So therefore immeasurable as you may be, Pete—address unknown notwithstanding—I choose to believe you are with me in every word that I write to you, even as I perceive that word in my consciousness before I scrawl it on to this paper. I rejoice in that faith. I want to see you again, hug you again, cry with you, hear your particular laugh, and the way you say, "Hey mom," "Hey dad." I want to drink micobrews with you again on some well-crafted sundeck. I cherish the conviction and refuse to allow the impossibility of your continuing life.

I just wish the hell you were still here.
Love, Dad

The Missing Voice

April 28—driving home from Portland

Dear Peter,

Jim said that when he got up early Monday morning and thought about my request for a family dinner that night instead of our normal immediate return to Bainbridge Island, he felt like it was a case of the patriarch calling the clan members in for a head count. I can hear your comments about me as the alpha male!

But Jim was right on target. As Jim and Tim and I stood around the grill on the patio, joined by Linda, I looked around a couple of times looking for whoever was missing. There was a voice, a mood, a point of view missing from the conversation. Even after I realized it was your voice that I was missing, I kept expecting it, missing it. How odd.

I was not alone in that feeling. When I got out of bed to get a drink of water, I found your sister Sarah, sobbing quietly, holding little Peter, with Jim holding her. I held them all for a while. "I loved Peter so," she sobbed. "He was always the bright one, the happy one. He brought a lightness. It will never be the same. I miss him so."

I didn't sleep very well. I've got a cold which snuck in over my shocked and weakened immune system. Mom greeted me with a warm good-morning hug. And as I carried a bag to the car in the rare early morning sunshine, I realized I was a little fearful about returning to Bainbridge Island and beginning to do routine things in a world without you.

Love, Dad

A With/Out World

April 29, Bainbridge Island

Dear Peter,

As you probably noticed, Peter, I'm running fast to catch up with routine things. A strange new world began April 6, with lots of covenants left over from the old one. I've been trying to get to some of them.

I finally hung the birdfeeders I bought a few days before the holy week of your death. It's a beautiful morning, but strange without your presence in it.

Without. With out. Even words look different now. Your with is out, Peter. Out with Peter's with.

Yet when I begin to do things like taking Yoshi for a walk or hanging a birdfeeder, I feel like I'm walking on a slight upgrade or into a headwind.

There is a power in your absence, Peter, just as there was a power in your presence. Even though your with is out.

Love, Dad

Comfort Food

April 30 On the way to Portland once more

Dear Peter,
While home on Bainbridge, Mom and I started reading through all the cards and letters. Beautiful. Astonishing. Persons we've not thought of for years are sending loving thoughts to us. One or another in an unpredictable way moves us to sobs. Again.

Dick's 90-year-old mother sent a three-line note: "When my grandson David was killed in a terrible auto accident, I could not cry. When I heard about Peter, I cried without control. May my tears be part of your healing."

Mom and I hold each other in turn when the sobs come.

O Peter, I don't want your death, I don't want, I don't want your death.

So here we are almost in Portland again. Coming to be with Linda—no, to be together on your tenth wedding anniversary today.

We are going to take Linda out to dinner with Tim and Sue, some fine place, to celebrate the day when she became part of our family.

Yes, we will celebrate. And probably cry. But celebrate that we can cry together.

We've also arrived a little early because yesterday your things arrived at Linda's new place from your apartment in Birmingham. We want to be around when Linda begins to open them.
Love, Dad

Sorrow Sweetened

May 1, On the way back to Bainbridge

Dear Peter,
I don't know how to begin today. There is so much I
want to say. This morning—the beginning of a new
month—dawned bright and warm and, for me, saddened. Sometimes it's just like that. Just a sad heaviness
shadowing everything.

It was some of the aftermath of yesterday I suppose.
We arrived at your house, and pulled into the driveway
and saw Linda cutting package tape and peering into the
big boxes containing all your things from your car and
from your apartment in Alabama. Our arrival was well
timed. Lynnea held Linda while she sobbed and sobbed.
And I held them both while they sobbed some more.

I was sad, but I didn't cry. Then. I think the sight of
all your clothes, golf clubs, business cards, Alabama tour
books (waiting for us); stuff from your desk, dresser,
bathroom and kitchen—all that simply stunned me into
a kind of disbelief again.

I suppose I needed to be disconnected for a while
from this new, overwhelming evidence of your recent
liveliness now dead.

I brought good clothes for the anniversary dinner, except I forgot my shoes. Good thing. Providence
of God. Somehow it helped to ask Linda permission,
laughingly granted, to root around in the boxes and find
a pair of your shoes, Pete, to wear to your tenth wedding
anniversary dinner celebration.

We went to this neat Italian restaurant. I joked that
you were missing another party and it served you right.
I sat at the head of the table with Mom and Linda on one
side and Tim and Sue on the other. I told the waiter I'd

take the check, but Linda grabbed the wine list and insisted on paying for the Chianti.

We clinked glasses and toasted Linda's tenth anniversary of becoming part of our family. Linda looked at her watch and observed that it was just about the time when you and she had promised to love forever.

It was a splendid evening with good food served family style. And that's what we were and still are. Mom and I are still marveling at the quality of the time, the conversation. We shared more deeply, warmly, of ourselves. There was lots of laughter.

It was a time different from any other, I think, and not only because of your absence, Peter. I told Mom this morning that it recalled for me Dominic Crossan's idea about the Resurrection of Jesus—his belief that even those followers of Jesus who did not see the empty tomb became believers in the Resurrection when they discovered that the power of Jesus to transform their relationships was still operative.

So perhaps for a while, we who grieve for you experienced in a way new to us the power of the Resurrection.

As I write now about last night, I find myself saying it was a 'sweet' time. Who was it at your memorial service, one of your colleague bosses who heard that somebody called you "Petey Pie"? And thereafter he always called you Petey Pie, because you were the sweetest guy he ever knew.

Love, Dad

One Too Soon, One Waiting

May 1, At home, later

Dear Peter,

I've already written—and you probably noticed anyway—that the day began sadly for me, perhaps because
the happiness of last night's gathering called from me
the hurt of your absence from it. Getting the paper in for
Jim and Sarah and loading the car again all seemed to
happen in slow motion.

Mom seemed upbeat, excited about leaving everything neat for Sarah and Jim, and discovering the direc-
tions for a shortcut to Starbucks! And so it is sometimes:
she cried yesterday and I didn't.

We went to see Dad. Fortunately he still knows us,
is glad to see us, smiles when I mention old times and
places, people; talks vaguely about community improve-
ments with a hint of the old social action preacher still
glowing within him. But conversation is sporadic. He
looks at the sky, the birds, the trees, more than at us. He
looks beyond.

Throughout our visit I felt more and more the hurt
of your loss, Peter, your sudden unnecessary death,
while my aging father waits patiently for his necessary
death. So when I walked out from his small care facility
onto the driveway the sobs that did not come yesterday
came today.

God, Peter, we miss you! Your never-again-ness,
your never-to-be-ness, evoked from me a high, thin wail
such as I've never heard from me since I was very little.
Mom held me and cried too.

Love, Dad

Your Shoes

May 5—At home, Bainbridge Island

Dear Peter,
I wore your other pair of shoes today, the black ones.
I did that wedding in a park up in Poulsbo. Weather
cleared nicely. The bride and groom had panicked when
they heard about you, thinking I might not be able to
do it. But I finally got around to calling them, and gave
them some reassurance.

I was pretty sure I could do it—that is, make it
through the service without falling apart. Falling apart
now and then (actually pretty often) is part of what will
eventually put us back together, but it would not work
well in the middle of a wedding service.

I really enjoy doing weddings—and I did enjoy
this one too. In this, the event was not so much under
the shadow of your death as in the light of your life and
death. It did give the service a different perspective,
hearing ". . . as long as we both shall live."

I felt a little odd wearing your shoes. When the
ceremony ended and as I was walking toward the food
table, I noticed that one shoe had come untied. As I put
my foot up on the bench and bent over to tie it, careful
not to droop my robe in the dirt, I clearly heard you saying with a laugh, "Hey Dad, need a little help tying my
shoe?"

Didn't you? Didn't I?
Love, Dad

The Other Side of the Dinner Table

May 3—Sunday, Bainbridge Island

Dear Peter,

It was difficult to decide where to go to church today, Pete. Our natural faith community would be Eagle Harbor Congregational. The retirement separation makes sense, facilitating the freedom of the congregation to develop rapport with a new pastor. But in our circumstances it also feels like an amputation.

We've worshipped at Bethany Lutheran Church several times. But we find the liturgy at Bethany a bother because all the fixed prayers rapidly recited leave so little time to pray. Yet Pastor Marty Dassler is a good friend, and the congregation has been so caring for us. Some came all the way to Portland for your memorial service. Just before you hit the tree, I'd done a month of Sunday Bible studies at Bethany. The church is only five minutes away from our house. So we went to the early service. Marty and others spotted us coming in at the last minute. Long, warm hugs. We needed them. Fortunately lots of people understand that.

And right off the bat, a line drive into our grieving hearts: many in the congregation were wearing Habitat T-shirts from their Adult Service adventure over in Yakima. That congregation does more than any I know to involve all ages in adventures in Christian service. "I got a chance to be Plaster Pastor Dassler," Marty quipped. His humor offers grace beyond the liturgical assurance. "It's really God building those Habitat Homes," he continued. Yes, and with you, Peter, right alongside enthusiastically pounding nails. I know Mom thought the same thing because she realized at that moment she had forgotten Kleenex. Fortunately, these days I keep some stashed in nearly every pocket.

The text from Acts told of Peter bringing Dorcas back to life. I hope Chelsey doesn't hear that one for a few years, since as you have surely noticed this is exactly what she thinks that God in all fairness should do for us, and you. Linda reports that Chelsey asks, "Why doesn't God?" at nearly every bedtime, often through her tears over how much she misses you.

I respect her question. While it's not practical granted limited real estate availability on the planet for God to bring back everybody, I too resent the notion of God picking favorites limited to the first century. If God is going to pick favorites, I agree with Chelsey that you should be among them. I really don't mess around much with those kinds of questions, but in Chelsey's suit against the Deity, I am *amicus curiae*.

Today was Mom's first communion in the new world, my second, with you on the other side of the table, so to speak. I must say, Pete, that your death has certainly pushed my theological limits. I am very much more aware of all those faith claims about communion here with all you saints in heaven there. I guess you noticed our tears indicating it was so for Mom and me this morning.

Of course the theological critic in me continues to be active, also, and more so. I had noticed the exuberant first grader in the children's choir who reminded me of you. And I was disappointed that although he and his peers knelt for a special blessing during communion, they didn't get to eat. What's a real family dinner without the kids? Especially Eucharist—thanksgiving dinner!

Maybe it was just as well since the bread offered is one of those pasty white wafers that taste like bathroom tissue dried after rolling into a wet sink. At least we dipped it in real wine instead of insipid Congregational grape juice, although even that didn't help much. Yes, I hear you chuckling about the contrast between this sterile stuff here and your hearty banquet on the other side of the table. If this were the only foretaste (foreplay?) of the heavenly banquet, I might be inclined to skip the heavenly climax. Okay, no smart remarks from you.

I love the language from the UCC Marriage Service which prays that the Holy Spirit may set us afire with love for God and make us "leap for joy" at God's presence at the banquet. Did you leap on the other side of this morning's dinner table, Pete? Some day in some kind of time I trust we'll all leap with joy for God, and for your presence face-to-face again. Meanwhile, we'll count each communion as a family dinner with you. Although frankly, Peter, I'd rather we were gathering with you for one of our family favorite breakfasts at Marco's Diner in Portland.

Love, Dad

Ultimate Adultery!

God-dammit, Peter, I'd like to put my face four inches from yours and yell and yell and yell and yell and yell! Jesus Christ, what a stupid way to die!

When we got to Linda's apartment for supper tonight, your death certificate was there on the kitchen counter. Linda watched Mom and me look at it.

"Contributing cause of death: acute ethanol intoxication."

"What a stupid choice," Linda said as she sat down at the head of the table.

Once, you will remember, I let you know in no uncertain terms that you'd better get the hell going with that marriage counseling, that your commitment to Chelsey demanded that you not stall, evade, or delay learning how to love each other. I wish—we all wish—that we'd have come down hard on your partying.

I was seduced like everybody else into thinking that your drinking was not that serious. I had never seen you drink and then drive. And I'd certainly never seen you drunk. It was only after you hit the tree that Mom and I began to hear that sometimes you really got blasted at parties.

Never a problem at work or home. Just at parties.

Shit. What the hell difference does that make now? Now you are also one of those stupid statistics that everybody knows and most everybody like yourself ignores, assuming they are the exception, immune to the odds.

So you partied at the home of Jim, your best friend, and Ann, his wife, celebrating that birdie on the last hole, so out of character from your usual golf that you fell on the green laughing and slapping the turf. Yes, and celebrating your anticipated triumphant appearance as an unbelievable financial success at your high school class reunion. And celebrating the arrival of Chelsey and Linda, just thirteen days away.

Damn. Damn. Damn. Damn. Damn. I noticed Linda cutting the asparagus and shaking her head. Booze in exchange for your life; what a helluva trade-off.

We all went to the condo pool. Kids had a great time. When I saw Linda splashing Chelsey and the cousins, I thought, she really is beautiful. I can certainly see why you cared for her so much—but not quite enough to care for your own safety.

Linda says she will have some things to say to Jim and Ann. I hope so. I've been picturing myself being gracious and forgiving. After all, you made your own decisions. But what kind of friend is it that does not try everything possible to protect a friend from the consequences of a bad decision?

I am going to propose to Jim and Ann that they get a handgun for the next party and just put a cartridge in the cylinder, give it a spin, and pass it around—instead of passing another round of drinks.

I didn't feel like eating. I don't feel like talking to anybody. I feel more tired than I've felt for a long time.

Jesus, Peter, why couldn't we see, you see, somebody see, that you were flirting with death?

You let yourself get seduced, Pete. Committed the ultimate adultery. No wonder we're all mad as hell.

Why? Why Didn't We?

May 11, The Day After Mother's Day

Dear Pete,
Yesterday your death shadow made all of us dark, each
of us in turn dealing with the fact that you were drunk
when you hit the tree. Sarah said it: "No dignity at all in
Pete's death."

And someday Chelsey will need to come to terms
with that fact too.

Yesterday I was so angry with you I could hardly
think of anything else. And then my anger expanded to
include the whole party culture. I'd like to rip Buffet's
"Margarita" song right out of the order of worship for
your memorial.

I am angry at us, at myself, for not catching on, not
noticing. I'd like to have hammered you with my words.
I wonder how long you've been on the edge. When did
you lose your judgment, Peter?

I remember when Tim decided long ago that he
could not drink while playing a gig if he wanted to play
good jazz. But for you, drinking was just part of the
party culture.

Your very good friend Jim and his wife, Ann, plan
to come back from Birmingham to visit with the family. I don't know how I will react to them. Jim was the
person most responsible for your move to the Compass
Bank. After golf together that fatal Sunday, you all
celebrated—barbeque, lots of enthusiastic conversation
about your astonishing final hole, the way Compass
Bank was taking off, Linda and Chelsey coming soon,
your anticipated triumphant return to your twenty-year
high school class reunion. Apparently you went around
Jim and Ann's house setting all the clocks ahead for
Daylight Saving time, and to make the time go faster.
And all the while pausing to help yourself to Jim and
Ann's booze.

Damn. I have some party proposals: Instead of olives in the martini, substitute rabbit turds. Maybe actual blood in the Bloody Mary? Piss in the pilsner? Those are just few of my imaginative ways of puncturing the ballooning denial to which we are all party when we party. If all else fails, puncture tires.

It's pretty crappy, Pete, to be thinking that one good thing about your death is that at least you didn't kill somebody else and survive yourself.

Mom just said that she wasn't sure she wanted just everybody to know you were drunk. She says not everybody will treat that information responsibly. She may be right. But I am not about to cooperate in a cover-up. Not anymore. We must have all been cooperating, enabling.

God, I hate the way your drunk death twists our grief. It shits on your whole life, Peter, and splatters on all of us. I am so disgusted with myself, with us, for not seeing, not warning. All the party turns sour. No heroism in your death, Pete. Who wants to hear another of the endless stories about dead drunks?

My grieving is soured, Peter. My tears are blocked with resentment. I don't feel like closing with "Love, Dad."
Dad

Trusting, toward Grace

May 11, later

Dear Peter,

Somewhere in his book, *Good Grief,* Granger Westberg says that "hostility is a bottomless pit." I don't want to muck around in it too long. I trust that healing grace will come. Perhaps it already has come, if I can be open to it.

Certainly, as you have probably noticed, we have experienced the strange blessedness of those who grieve.

Do you notice, Peter? Are you there, Peter? I face the reality that the fact of your drunk death has some-how diminished my sense of your aliveness, and that saddens me even more.

Each time we have come back home to Bainbridge, people have picked us up, hugged us, cried with us, fed us, listened to us talk about you endlessly. Now we will need to add the embarrassing end of the story. But the grace, the comfort will still be there, I'm sure.

Last week two astonishing things happened which want to pull us into a future which seems good and bright even without you, Peter. For the first time ever, your Mom got to meet her cousin, Chris, from Australia. Chris and her husband, Frank (during sabbatical work at UW), ended up staying with us for four nights. Almost immediately Mom and her cousin Chris were enjoying each other like long lost sisters! It was a discovery of a new family, new love. We want to visit their family in Perth, and sometime explore Swedish roots together.

And incredibly, we suddenly have money with which to do it. A bequest came, completely unexpected. Maybe you remember how thirty-plus years ago in St. Louis, Pauline Lacatour always said she was going to remember me in her will, because I helped her disabled daughter, Minette, find good friends in Hope Church.

Minnette died, too young, in a fire. Pauline died at age 102, and notice of her bequest to me came last week.

Grace happens. I want to be open to it, Pete.
Love, Dad

Embraced

May 11, At home, still later

Dear Peter,

We came home to still more letters and a phone message from my longtime friend, my other college roommate, Reine Abele. Last week I had written him a short note about your death.

Reine spoke slowly obviously struggling for words. He and his wife, Elsa, had remembered us in prayer at church that morning. He'd been to a performance of Mendelssohn's *Elijah* in the afternoon and remembered that we had sung it together at Elmhurst. He said he thought of us when he heard again, "Cast your burden upon the Lord, and he shall sustain you."

His timing was right. I put my head in my hands and sobbed a long time.

I felt again that you were sobbing with me, Pete. And that a Comforter was embracing both of us.

Love, Dad

Sob-Kicks, Birth Pangs

May 12, at home

Dear Peter,

As you've probably noticed, we are amazed by the way the gut-punching reality of your death hits us again and again. Different times, different ways, but often surprising.

Here is Mom suddenly sobbing as she hangs up the phone. What's happened? She's called the phone company to explain why she is late paying the bill. "It hurts so much to say it—that our son has been killed."

She sobbed a long time and I held her like she held me yesterday.

I admire her courage as a bereaved mother. I told her as I held her that feeling the sob-kick in her stomach muscles made me think of how she worked those same muscles to thrust you into the world four hours before church that Sunday May 15th morning, thirty-eight years ago two days after tomorrow.

We love you, Peter. And miss you.

Love, Dad

Elegant Elephant

May 15, at home, bedtime, after a banquet

Dear Peter,
It was an elegant dinner at Seattle University. Mom looked gorgeous in that stunning black dress she bought at discount after modeling it. Remember?

I enjoyed the time. People there are sensitive enough to say things that bring tears, and they understand the tears, and sometimes they tear with us.

Coming home, our good friend Lee Fickle admired our Saturn station wagon. We told him how you helped us check out the price. Then pulling into our garage, I recalled with Mom how you suddenly appeared at the dealership in your dark blue business suit (same shoes I wore tonight) with a way to finance the car that would be better for both for us and for Dad.

Likewise, your sister and brother will be making payments for quite a while on some fine financial transactions that you arranged.

Sitting in the car, Mom said, "It hurts so much to think we'll never see him simply appear like that again." And later, getting ready for bed, "I remember coming down early in my p.j.s, and Peter was already up. We had a cup of coffee together. It was such a good time. He was such a good son." Just thought you'd like to know, Pete.
Love, Dad

P.S. One more thought, Peter, about tonight's elegant dinner. Fine white wine. One glass with appetizers. Some people had two. Then two glasses with dinner.

I thought of my party proposals. But this was an elegant party.

It's like there is an elephant among us. Invisible. But powerfully present. Sometimes it is an elegant elephant, warm, appreciative, celebrative. Sometimes it is a circus elephant full of clowning and play. But at heart it's a rogue elephant. If you don't watch it carefully, it smashes heads. Right, Pete?

Left With Blameless Grief

After a week in Portland, driving back to Bainbridge

Dear Peter,

I am a little reluctant to write. I am shy of the pain that comes when I concentrate on you. And when I write while Mom drives, she is left alone.

As you probably know, a lot has happened in the past three days. Your friends Jim and Ann flew back from Birmingham to meet with all the family. We gathered at Sarah and Jim's home for dinner. At first we stood around with a glass of wine and hardly talked about you at all unless I made a point of it. I was impatient. Finally, late in the dinner, Jim and Ann began to talk about you and your last day. They confirmed that you were so exuberant that last night—the great golf game, Linda and Chelsey soon to come, anticipating that class reunion back in DeKalb. "They will never believe that I'm earning a six-figure salary!"

Linda broke into tears when she heard that report.

And then they laughed telling how you ran around the house setting all the clocks ahead. You were so happy and so full of the future. You'd occasionally fixed a drink for yourself throughout the evening. You ate steak ravenously, probably because you'd been on a crash diet, trying to lose weight and win a bet with Linda. You'd been working six days a week, coming into the office at five a.m., going home at seven p.m., getting everything ready for Linda and Chelsey. There was absolutely no indication that you would have any trouble driving back to your apartment, just five minutes away.

The police came to Jim and Ann's home the next day, and asked about their entire day with you. Apparently skid marks indicated that you had not fallen asleep. Something else happened, they suspect. A deer. Or perhaps something dropped from the dashboard, the videocassette perhaps. Linda with tears told of two videos that had been shipped back with your things from the car. One was crushed.

So we are left again with sudden, accidental death. And not knowing. And not blaming.

Anybody. Not you, either Pete.

I am embarrassed about what I wrote before, when I was so angry.

We deeply appreciate the evening with Jim and Ann. Obviously they are also grieving.

They loved you. Jim says he just cannot bring himself as yet to recruit a replacement for you. And every day, they drive past the tree.

I feel more at peace with your death, in that there seems to be no particular negligence which caused it. Except perhaps your habitual neglect of the seatbelt. So we are now left with simple grief.

The task of getting Dad's financial stuff transferred from you to Tim took me to the Pac One Bank where I last saw you at work when we were buying the car. It was heavy, sitting there where you had been such an enthusiastic presence. Your former co-workers were kind and helpful. Friday afternoon—your birthday—I sat with Linda while she talked with a financial advisor, one of your peers. At least financially—thanks to the large death benefits you never expected to be needed, Linda will be secure for the rest of her life. I am very glad. It's going to be tough enough anyway.

All the family gathered at the Market Pub. Bob and Debbie and their two kids joined us. As you probably know, they are committed to doing something with Linda and Chelsey every Friday night until . . . who knows? It was a wild, raucous time, good beer, great hamburgers (a Greek special with kalamata olives and feta cheese), kids chasing each other under the tables. You would have loved it for a birthday party, Pete. Jim said he thought of you all the time we were there, and heard your hearty chuckles as we took turns trying to corral the rambunctious kids.

Chelsey must have thought of you too. When we gathered again for breakfast this morning, Linda reported that while we were leaving the Market Pub Friday night, Chelsey sobbed on the parking lot: "I want my Daddy!" Linda said Chelsey has not cried so hard since seeing your body at your memorial service. Even though we know it's healthy grief for Chelsey and all of us, we hate it.

Love, Dad

Everything, Everything Different

Sunday, May 17, 11 PM, at home on Bainbridge

Dear Peter,
Six weeks ago at this time you were already dead and we
didn't know it. And I still don't believe it. I still find myself shaking my head a lot. I always want to look at your
picture. We need to put some more around our house so
we can see you wherever we are.

Last week, Jim and Sarah showed us a bit of video
from that great weekend you and Jim and Ann arranged
for us at Sun River. We watched you pushing the kids on
sleds. Great shots of the kids. But we wanted to see more
of you. You'd count to three and give them a big shove,
and then the camera would move away from you, of
course, and follow the kids. Sometimes you are just on
the edge of the frame. Sometime we hear you laughing,
cheering, but we can't see you.

Oh Peter, I am so sad. Not crying. Just sad.

Last night the Deineses and Cunninghams invited
us to go see the film *Horse Whisperer*. As you know, it
is always hard for us to come back, to pull away from
Linda and Chelsey again. But every time someone has
been here to pick us up and carry us away from the loneliness of our grief.

Horse Whisperer is a wonderful film about healing.
And about accepting the fact of an accident. Healing
grief.

Mom has cried often these past few days. Lisa, your
good friend from high school, called on your b.d., left a
message that she was thinking of us. Mom cried when
we played it.

Dear, dear Peter, we love you so. You were so easy
to love, so warm to be with. We miss you and anticipate
missing you. And yet it seems so unreal. The books
we've bought about grief—for Chelsey or with Chelsey

in mind—we have them here, yet half the time I can hardly believe they are here because of you.

We just love you so. I keep imagining your voice, and sometimes I try to imitate your laugh. We love your gentle way of teasing, of encouraging. God, Peter, what a hole, what an emptiness! You have been such a gift. I just don't want it to end. I don't want it all in the past tense. I want another 30 years of you for me and Mom, another 60 for Linda and Chelsey.

Everything, everything, seems different, *is* different. I can't quite describe what it is or how it is, but it is absolutely a different world—in the way it feels and looks.

Peter. Pete. Pete.

Love, Dad

Peter. Peter. Peter. Peter. Peter. Mom held me while I sobbed for a while. We held each other and cried for a while. She wants you around for a long time yet too.

Crossing Over, Crossing Back

Wednesday, May 20, on the ferry after Jazz Service

Dear Peter,

I brought stuff along to look over in preparation for the class I will begin teaching in the fall term at the School of Theology and Ministry. But I feel more like writing to you. I guess I just need to keep tending to my grief work, Pete!

Mom and I went to the Wednesday noontime jazz service at Plymouth—Feed Your Soul At Lunchtime, we call it. Superb! Great jazz trio—vibes, piano, and bass. You would have loved it! In our last phone conversation you talked about jazz in Birmingham.

Tony's sermon was likewise superb: close to the text, close to life. And I love singing from the *New Century Hymnal*: "Everything's gonna be alright." Sort of broke me up. "I've been talking to Jesus about it; everything's gonna be alright." Was it a message from you, Pete?

Then in Tony's prayer—"for those in sudden, stunning grief." How strange it was that after months of talking about getting together with Tony and his wife, Linda, we finally happened to catch a lunch with them after church just a few hours before you were killed. Tony was the first person to call us that day. Today was the first time we have seen him since. Long, long, quiet hug. Embrace. Quiet tears.

Then Mom and I went to lunch at the Palomino. It's fun to do something classy in the city once in a while. I noticed again how at any time either of us may be head down, or eyes far off, unfocused, invariably thinking of you.

Mom went off to her board meeting at First Hill Learning Center, so I'm by myself on the ferry. And I just met Anna Bell, back from UTexas. She is such a beautiful, bright spirit. She had her own horrid encounter with sudden death last year when the mudslide up by Rolling Bay took out the whole family for whom she'd babysat a few hours before it struck.

Characteristically, she is now concerned for us: "Anything I can do to help? Bring something by? Do some chores?"

"Not that I can think of—but we'd like to see you. We'd like to talk about Peter."

"I'd like to hear about him."

A hug.

Tonight, after I pick up Mom, I'll stop by Steve's to consult over a beer with him and Eric about the upcoming weekend male-bonding overnight backpack. Still lots of snow around. I can't imagine we'll hike to anyplace very high. The guys have been very urgent about including me in the outing. I appreciate that. The wives will take good care of your mom.

A week from today we will fly to L.A. with Linda and Chelsey. Several months ago Mom and I had planned to visit my Uncle Carl and his wife, Wilma, at their beautiful home in the Garner Valley Ranch above Palm Springs. Now it just seems right to bring Linda and Chelsey along. We'll visit your Uncle Karl in Whittier, too.

Miss you, Pete.

Dad

P.S. On the ferry coming over (as you may have observed) I ran into a guy whose behavior at times I did not appreciate, and I had not especially cared to see him again. But in this morning's encounter, he was most attentive and kind. Moved me to tears. Sometimes, God is not subtle at all. Have you noticed?

Stretching for Both Sides

May 21, waiting at the ferry terminal
Dear Peter,
I figure I might as well get off a few lines to you while
I wait for Mom to get me from the ferry. I probably
should have been a little more specific about time and
place!

I enjoyed a fine morning meeting with the
Advisory Board at the School of Theology and Ministry
at Seattle University. The last ninety minutes were especially good, sitting in on a lunch with four STM Roman
Catholic grads that were telling faculty and administra-
tion about how STM had prepared them for ministries
in the Catholic Church. All lay ministers, of course.
Often they find a difficult tension between the bright
open exploration of the School and the closed, fearful,
and controlling institutional Church. Lots of pain, but
also lots of fulfillment.

It is such a privilege to be in on that kind of conversation. It is such a gift to have some part in the shaping
of what may be (a century from now?) a new kind of
church. STM is the only place in the world, as far as we
know, which is founded to be intentionally ecumenical,
with Roman Catholic students and students from ten
participating non-Catholic denominations studying all
core curriculum side-by-side. And, every student learns
about every other faith tradition in a course named
"Theology in an Ecumenical Setting." Actually in the
process, each also learns much more about their own!

When one adds the Jesuit concern for social justice,
grounded in Jesuit spiritual formation, it is not surprising that our UCC students feel right at home. Really, it
feels to me like the continuing development of values
that are at the heart of our UCC church family, Pete. I'm
loving it!

Once again Peter, I have that extreme contrast between a wonderful feeling of blessedness on one side,
and on the other side the totally sad reality of your
death. It is very hard to get my head and heart around
both sides. But certainly the STM community and my
involvement in it is a part of the comfort which is provided to those of us who grieve your death. I am grateful
for it.
Love, Dad

Valley of the Sour

May 22, coming home on the ferry

Dear Peter,

"Let's try not to be so sour about things," Mom said as she took me to the ferry.

I was sour this morning. Last night our good contractor friend Steve saw for himself what Mom had warned him about: we need a wider base for the relocated wood stove. We wanted that done before our video group comes Sunday night. Now we won't make it.

"Tell the gang we can't host," I groused. "Call Hoffmans and tell 'em they'll need to do it instead of us."

Mom was sour about my sour orders. I was sour anyway because the woodstove project with its beautiful solid cherry mantel (a gift from Steve and Barbara) is part two of the custom-crafted, floor-to-ceiling cherry bookshelf and cabinets on the wall opposite the woodstove. It is the project about which we kept saying, "Wait 'till Peter sees this! He'll appreciate it more than anyone else in the family."

It was to be the year of the woodstove/bookshelf/living room renewal.

It was to be the year of the garden. My first year of retirement, so I'd have more time, right? Plans. Rhododendrons purchased at bargain prices but still in the pots. And I'm still in the pits, Pete. Because you died. Sour about that, too.

The guys got me to go on this overnight backpack tomorrow. I've been grousing about that, to myself and Mom, not to them, hoping we get rained out so I can get the rhodies out of the pots and into the ground, and clean up some of the yard. It's a neglected mess because we've been all the time running to Portland so that we can grieve with the rest of the family. I'm behind in correspondence. I'm behind in my reading I need to do in order to plan my course in fall.

Sour morning. Sour me. Yea, I walk through the valley of the Sour.
Love anyway, Dad

**Wednesday, May 27,
departure from Portland to L.A.**

Dear Peter,
How are you doing? What's it like, Pete? If we could hear
you, could you describe it? Or is your reality beyond the
ability of language to convey? I think so. I believe that
you are still essentially you, enhanced, healed by the
grace of God, but anything more than that is beyond my
capacity to imagine, and likewise indescribable to me.
Poetry and metaphor reach toward your present life by a
different route.

It's been a while since I've had a chance to write.
I am frustrated about that since I am always mentally
composing a letter to you. Life continues to have that
double perspective—events happen, and events happen
in the perspective of your death. Everything. Everything
continues to be shadowed. Around our house especially,
I feel like I am walking through a demolished and only
partially reconstructed area.
This was to be the year of the garden—did I write
this already? All is overgrown. Disheveled. Rhodies
we bought before you were killed are still in the pots.
Others and azaleas which came as tribute to you and
comfort to us are still not planted. And the woodstove
project is still not done. I'm angry with the guy whom
we asked to design it. The design he gave us looks like he
just didn't care. So we and Steve are trying to make the
guy's mistake look good.
Partly for that reason, Monday was a dreary day,
saddened by the memory of your death inside and outside the house. I am still sour, irritated at everything. It
was sunny and warm for a while in the afternoon so I
suggested we eat an early supper outside on your deck.
But by the time we got out there it was cloudy and cold

again. The whole day I felt as if I was paddling upstream in a polluted creek. I wanted to write, but there was too much to do and I was too tired.

Now it's Wednesday morning and we are on our way to L.A. with Linda and Chelsey, but I still feel about the same. As I said earlier, we planned this trip months ago. At the moment, I have little enthusiasm for it. But it is something we need to do, Peter, especially for Chelsey—to keep life exciting and interesting for her, with people who love her. In spite of your death.

Love, Dad

Close Encounter

May 27, in flight, Portland to L.A.

Dear Peter,
We checked our bags at curbside. Chelsey engaged the porter in conversation just like you would have done at the same age.

"Do you know what?"

"No, what?" he smiled.

"My daddy died." Linda smiled down at Chelsey and put her hand on Chelsey's shoulder.

"Oooh, I'm sorry. What happened?"

"He was killed in an accident."

"Oh, that's too bad. I bet you miss him a lot."

Chelsey smiled and nodded.

Did you notice all that, Pete? I think you must be especially close in such encounters.

Love, Dad

Adventure Recall, Emptied Dreams

May 27, later, in flight

Dear Peter,

Well, it was a great overnight backpack after all! Just right for an early start on the season, and a wonderful initiation for Allan, his first such venture. I lent him my old JanSport pack, the one we bought in Kirkwood twenty-seven years ago; remember? And that campsite in the meadow below the Rio Grande Window, with its sudden, spectacular vista of the whole western range of the San Juans! It was the target for church backpack adventures for years, and none better than the summer all three of you kids joined it. The final night campfire photo of us thirteen triumphant flat-landers is prominent on our family wall of memories.

As I had expected, there was still too much snow to hike high this past weekend, so it was a fairly leisurely, valley camping experience. For me there was that same double vision: beautiful, hilarious—and therefore also filled with reminders of your death.

I remembered all the times backpacking with you and Mom and Tim and Sarah, and told some of the stories. When the guys hung food packs, I simply had to tell them what happened to us in Yosemite on our first backpack; remember? You and Tim spent all that time looking for the right two trees between which to stretch the line (as the ranger had instructed us to do)—and the next morning we discovered that momma bear and her cub had found it anyway. I recited for the guys the children's sermon I wrote about that adventure. "It is said, Little Bear," said Mom Bear proudly, "that man has dominion over the earth—but we Bears are still in charge of Little Yosemite Valley!"

And I told about that first night in Grand Canyon when you and I snickered at Mom's claim that some creature was trying to get into our tent—and later we woke to your panicked yell when the mouse found the peanuts in the pocket of the shirt you wore in your sleeping bag!

I thought a lot about that last hike you did with Mom and me up the Gore Ridge Trail into the lovely Alpine Lakes Wilderness. I remembered how you and I explored a spectacular hidden waterfall.

So the whole overnight was great fun with the guys and at the same time filled with the heavy presence of your forever absence, Peter, the never-again-ness of your presence. I think that is why I was so sad all of Monday.

Cards, phone calls, continue to come from people who have only just heard about your death. Mom and I are always being asked how we are. It all helps, especially when the person asking seems to really want to know, and seems to simply accept whatever we want to say.

At STM, Julie Davis caught me in the office while waiting for the Board meeting. She knows how to ask and how to listen for a response. I talk about trying to be open to good grieving. We talked for maybe twenty minutes. For most of that time I was smiling and weeping. If we'd been less public, I probably would have been once again convulsed with sobs.

At the same time—this seems so odd—I find myself shaking my head when I remind myself that you are dead. It is still so hard to believe. That so suddenly when everything was going so well for you, for the whole family, suddenly you are out of it. Forever.

And now we are one of those families who have lost a son. Whose son was killed. For all these years, that was always something that happened, although rarely, to somebody else. Sure, we sometimes grieved with them, but it was not us. It still is hard to believe it is us this time. Like Mom said this morning, "When I see Linda and Chelsey" (without you, Pete), "it is really hard." Love, Dad

Tears and Laughter

June 4, on return flight, L.A. to Portland

Dear Peter,

A few moments ago we flew over Yosemite with Half Dome clearly visible. It's amazing how much I am moved by seeing it. How old were you when we made that hike, Pete, eleven? Mom, Tim, and I left you and Karl at the base of the Half Dome cables because it simply looked too terrifying for you two. And then this young teacher, whom we happened to meet just as he came down, coached and wooed you both all the way to the top. You suddenly appeared over the rim just as we were about to descend. What a glorious reunion! I've got a fantastic photo of you and Karl perched on top that lizard's-head outcrop with nothing but thousand of feet of air beneath you. God, what a day that was!

We've had a fine time with Linda and Chelsey, just wonderful. What a gift to be able to spend so much time with just the two of them. Chelsey is a marvelous five-year-old. So imaginative. Waiting in line at Disneyland, she never seemed bored. Here she is waiting for the Rocket Ride, making funny faces at me thirty feet away. Never whined the whole trip. She is constantly inventing games to engage one of us. Or in a pretend mode all by herself. In restaurants she takes the role of pouring wine or taking our orders for dessert, with great attention to realistic, dramatic detail.

Linda is marvelous with her, playing along most of the time, very clear and courteously firm when she has had enough, and laughing heartily at Chelsey's antics.

And Chelsey is every bit as engaging with strangers as you were at that age. And she has that slight overbite like you had. Once when I carried her up to the motel room because she was barefoot, I had this strong strange warm feeling that I was carrying you, Pete.

Then there is the shadowed dimension of this trip. It seems surreal to spend so much time with Linda and Chelsey and without you. So unreal. I still can't believe you are dead, Pete.

Sometimes at night or when I'm alone for a while, I replay in my head Tim's phone call and his opening words: "Dad, I have some very, very, very bad news. Peter was killed tonight."

I still can't get it, Pete. Don't want to get it.

Tomorrow you will have been dead for two months. I find myself checking the calendar again. Only two months. Weird. I can't get it that you are dead and yet it seems like it was a half year since Tim called. I feel bad about not being with Linda and Chelsey on this two-month observance.

I have such vivid images of you, Peter; so easily they come to me. Does that have anything to do with your existence now?

It is an enormous comfort to trust that you are alive, sentient, aware, observing, remembering, responding, accompanying us, laughing and crying with us. I can't stand the thought of you not existing somehow as you. You being absent, your absent being, is bad enough.

There were so many powerful moments in the past eight days. I didn't get a chance to write, so I made a few notes. Like Monday night, we all did a barbeque in La Mirada Park. While the chicken was grilling, Linda and Chelsey and Karl were playing soccer about thirty yards away. It was just dusk, a gorgeous sunset, and they were silhouetted against the ripening peach sky, just far enough away so that all I could hear was their laughter and an occasional shout. God, it was beautiful. And what made it so powerful is indicated by the fact that when I started to write about it just now, I was saying in my head "You, and Linda and Chelsey playing . . ." You, Pete. God how I wish . . .

You witnessed, I presume, Chelsey's big grin when Uncle Carl lifted her on to his quarter horse, Spinit. Mom says she wishes she could have seen your smile at that moment. Spinnet got royal treatment from Chelsey—four times his usual ration of carrots. "Your Daddy would be so proud of the way you rode Spinnet," I said. Chelsey immediately burst into tears. Linda held her.

Chelsey cried in church Sunday before the prayer time when some mom asked for prayers for her son, badly hurt in an auto accident. So did Linda. But later Chelsey joined the Sunday school kids in a "Happy Birthday, Church" song for Pentecost. Then she was up front with the rest of the kids smiling, singing, and bobbing her helium balloon.

At the park, while Chelsey was entertaining herself in the sand, and on the climber-slide, I told Linda how much I appreciated the way she allowed Chelsey to cry and to be happy. And then I held Linda while she sobbed. And Mom held us both.

One thing missing from our time was more direct conversation with Linda about how Linda is doing. Another time, Pete. We're doing the best we can for them.

Love, Dad

P.S. That glorious reunion on top of Half Dome—the next time you'll be waiting for us; right, Pete?

Releasing the Toboggan

June 6, returning from Portland to Bainbridge

Dear Peter,
"This is always a sad time," I said to Sarah this morning,
"leaving Portland, going home."

Mom agrees. Sarah says she always hates to see us
go. We all hold each other. Mom and Sarah cried.

The family hates more separations, Pete. For the
first time in her life, Mom is afraid of a loss, another loss
in the family. Being together helps us to talk about your
absence while still being comforted by each other's presence.

I am hungry for a recent picture of you. Sarah has
one from the family weekend you arranged in Sun River,
the last time we saw you. In the photo you are bending
over Chelsey on the red toboggan, just releasing her
down the little hill.

Releasing her. Releasing her. Too soon. Too soon.

Mom teared up as we drove up I-5 along the
Willamette River, remembering your love of the boat,
(the last time we talked, you'd found a berth for the boat
in Birmingham) and that wonderful day last summer
when we took it almost all the way up to where Chelsey
and Linda are now living.

We pass intersections where we used to turn toward you. "Portland is filled with Peter," Mom says.
Marco's, Bank of America, the Market Pub . . .

Last night I awoke with this startling, clear image of
you smiling. God, you were so real! Yet so untouchable.
Likewise Mom, last week sometime, woke with what she
describes as a brilliant blue light followed by you, saying,
"I'm okay!" "But," she says, "we're not okay yet, Peter."

Do you already know how it will be for us, too,
Peter? That it will be okay? Are you so confident now of

the loving care of God that you know it will be okay for us too? We are not there yet, Pete. Of course, its only two months today. 61 days. But I don't think the idea of you getting killed will ever be okay. A lot of remarkable, even miraculous things may happen in spite of your death, "more than we ever dare to ask or even imagine"—but nothing, nothing, will ever compensate for your loss. Nothing.

Yet we will not be closed to joy and laughter. Perhaps we will see Linda married again, and a new loving father for Chelsey. And I will try my damndest to live to see Chelsey's firstborn. I trust all that, I hope for all that. But I will never stop not wanting your death.

Dammit Peter, you were just taking off in a new venture, and you were more valued, more highly regarded by your peers than we ever came close to realizing. A new chapter, the first chapter in a new volume of your life story, had just begun—and suddenly the page went blank. We will now never know how it might have turned out for you. But besides that—and more important—we just miss you and your unique way of loving all of us.

Mom says that Linda has written letters of appreciation and news for all of your friends. She includes a warning about the dangers of the particular ways you all partied. A gutsy thing to do, I think—to recognize the endlessly repeated consequences of drinking and driving. Whether or not your party drinking that day caused your death, it certainly didn't help.

So here we are on the road back to Bainbridge. We miss Linda and Chelsey. We won't see them until June 21 when they come up for the tree planting in your memory at Eagle Harbor Church. That will be a good event, I think. But we will miss you and miss you and miss you all summer long.

I wonder how often thirty years from now Chelsey will ponder that picture of you shoving her off on the toboggan.

Love, Dad

P.S. As you have seen, Pete, I write these letters and then when there is a chance to do so, I read them to Mom. And we both cry.

Remember that woodcarving of the rocking Madonna? We gave it to Mom one Christmas. You were about six or eight. And with it a note reading, "This is the kind of a mom you wanted. This is the kind of a mom we think you are."

She is a super mom; right, Pete? I was thinking today, this morning, dammit, it just should not have happened to her. If I didn't think that God agrees that it should not have happened to her, I might become a very sour old man.

All Praise to God with Wounded Hearts

June 16, at home, Bainbridge

Dear Pete,

I am sitting here in sunshine on your deck (your concept, your labor, with me pounding some nails). I am waiting for the umbrella to dry, so I can apply enough tape to the slide to keep it open for the season. You remember the latch broke about six months after we bought it. I knew you'd get a charge out of me repairing it with duct tape! Actually clear, tough package tape works better and looks better. You are probably suggesting that since the umbrella mechanism broke after only six months, it was a bad deal to start with, and since with taped assistance we've used in now for twelve years, maybe we could afford to break for a new umbrella. Maybe so.

We're working hard to get our house and grounds ready for the big day Sunday—the tree planting in your memory at Eagle Harbor Church. The congregation invited the whole community, placing very nice advertisements in the *Bainbridge Review*.

So, naturally, Tim, Sue, Miles, Erin, and Jim, Sarah, Hannah, Peter, and Linda and Chelsey will be up for the weekend. We trust that you will be with us, Peter, even though there is a microbrew festival on the other side of the Sound with 152 different tastes available!

Father's Day. First time "our kids" (as Mom and I unwittingly call you all) will be with us here since you were killed.

I write these words "since you were killed" and I realize I am shaking my head again. The other day walking our ever-faithful retriever, Yoshi, I was thinking of you and I found I had clenched my teeth, hard.

I still don't want to take it in, Pete, the fact that you are so suddenly, irreversibly, needlessly gone. I get the strange feeling often that I wish you and I had talked it over before you died—your death, that is, so I could have convinced you it was really not a good idea.

So I look to the weekend coming as another time of great joy and great pain. I'm delighted that everybody will be here. Except that not everybody will be here.

We'll be showing off the exquisite cherry wood floor-to-ceiling bookshelf and cabinets with matching cherry mantle over the woodstove opposite. But it is you, Peter, who would most appreciate the workmanship. The heavy presence of your absence will hang around all our time together.

Sometimes the better things are, the worse they are. Like the other night at the performance of the High School Vocal Jazz group. We went because the McComb kids are in it. Top-notch group! The more we enjoyed it, the more we missed you. Our applause mixed with our tears.

Walter Brueggemann wrote again to us, speaking of our "days of endless loss."

Dick Ellerbrake wrote yesterday that your death must have opened the old wounds from the loss of their David, born the same year as you, killed in an accident, twenty years before you. "Ever present anguish," he said.

We appreciate such comments from such persons, "acquainted with grief" in their own experience, especially when it is clear that they somehow manage to focus on us, in spite of their own lingering pain.

I'm sad, Pete. One text in worship today was from Ps. 42. During my dark winter in the sawmill long ago, it was a life-saver for me. "Why art thou cast down, oh my soul? I shall again praise Him, my Help and my God." Yes, we praise God—especially for all the sensitive love and comfort with which we have been surrounded. But it's not the same. Hearty praise but with a wounded heart.

Love, Dad

Tree Planting and the Cousin Factor

June 23, on the ferry to Seattle

Dear Peter,

I just said goodbye with hugs and kisses to the all the family. As we expected, everybody came up for yesterday's Tree Planting—the cherry tree planted at Eagle Harbor Church in your memory, Pete.

After breakfast at the Bluewater Diner, I got dropped off at the ferry. And so I am into the sadness of departure and separation. With family, it is always more weighted now. Like taffy, we hate to be pulled apart. Like the loaf, we resist the breaking. It is always a little hurt, rubbing the still raw scab of the big hurt.

But it was a splendid weekend! Best ever, Sarah said. Perfect weather, warm and clear. We took the retirement gift kayak to Pleasant Beach and everybody got a chance to ride.

The Tree Planting at first had a strangeness about it. When we approached the spot where everybody had gathered on the church lawn, it looked almost like a year ago when we all gathered there for my retirement party—the last time you were here on Bainbridge Island, Peter.

Beautiful prayer, reflections, music. All the church-school children and our family moving to the cherry tree to add soil from our gardens. Our friends Bob and Lynne sent soil from their farm in Missouri. Chelsey added some of your ashes. A couple hundred people came, I guess. Lots of hugs, tears, long lingering conversations. Beautiful.

Then home for grilled steaks and microbrews on your deck. You missed it again, Pete!

After the kids went to bed, we sat for a long time in the Adirondack chairs, on the longest day of the year, sitting and talking quietly through twilight and starlight, warming our feet with the citronella candles. Beautiful.

We talked about the moods, moves, times, and forms of our grieving for you. Jim was holding little Peter on his lap. "Oh, Peter," he said, "Who could ask for a better Father's Day gift than you!" Whereupon, Linda burst into tears. Mom held her while she sobbed. We were simply quiet together for a while.

Then we turned to stargazing. Jim is great at pointing out the constellations.

He called our attention to Cygnus. Everybody looked up—and suddenly a meteor burst out of it. "Peter!" everybody said at once. I wonder if somehow, somewhere, our half-facetious act of recognition could be more true than anyone of us "dare to ask or even imagine."

Last night Miles and Chelsey snuggled into the bunk beds so tickled to be sleeping next to each other. At their ages, five and four, they are great buddies.

Before bedtime last night we gave them each a squishy clear plastic toy containing a weird creature floating in some liquid. When Chelsey dropped hers on the sidewalk, it broke. Chelsey exploded in tears. Immediately Miles gave her his—a pretty good act of compassion for a four-year-old, or at any other age for that matter. It made me recall how you and I talked about the possible loss of the cousin factor in your move away from Portland to Birmingham; remember? The cousin factor is even more important now, and we will continue to nurture it.

I put a new rope on the tire swing. Chelsey and Miles loved it. "Miles, you know who put up this tire swing? Your uncle Pete."

"Yeah, but he died."

Right to the point, huh, Pete?

And that is why we continue to do our best, Peter, to do everything we can to make things beautiful and fun and loving, in order to protect ourselves from the ever-present pain of your endless absence.

Love, Dad

From One of Our Comforters: Poetry

PETER'S TREE

The sapling cherry's leaves jitter
in a breeze that stirs
but does not cool the air.
Risky to plant a tree in June

for the young man we mourn, lost
when his car swerved off the road.
A wife and five-year old survive,
Sobs clog his family's throats.

Circling the tree's base, children
in summer shirts, dresses, bright
as flowers, pour out their jars
of garden dirt, pat down, hands used
to making sand pies on the beach.

In the daughter's dark hair, a bow,
brave purple, bobs. Too young
to understand, she carefully blends
ashes with the soil.

Beneath the family huddled in chairs
beneath old firs, we friends can offer
arms, like branches, to shelter, share
the grief. Come spring, we'll watch
for the assurance of new green,
the promise of white blossoming.

—*Pat Loken*

A Thank-You Letter to the People
of Eagle Harbor Church

Dear Friends,

Lynnea and I want to express our profound thanks for the Service of Tree Planting for our son Peter. The service was a beautiful culmination of the outpouring of loving care for us and our family from all of you and the Bainbridge Island community since the word spread of Peter's sudden death, April 5.

We are amazed by all the notes and letters, phone calls, flowers, visits, hugs, conversations, prayers, meals, help with chores, contributions to Habitat for Humanity, and a multitude of kindnesses which continue to come to us. Just as it is impossible for us to express adequately our sense of loss for Peter, so it is also impossible to express adequately our gratitude for all the acts of caring from you. Truly, how blessed are those who grieve; the faith community brings God's comfort more abundantly than we could ever have imagined.

The Tree Planting for Peter was a lovely expression of all of that. In particular we want to say thank you to Peter Maitland and Tad Sakuma and any others for their wise attention to the tree; to Francis Roberts for the lovely flowers from her garden; to Carol Thornburgh for words of faith from the Scriptures; to Michelle Bombardier for such sensitive articulation of our thoughts and feelings in prayer; to all the children who brought earth from their own gardens and played with Chelsey after the service; to Bill Edmonds and Rick Ridgeway for "Amazing Grace;" to Rita Rowe for the sounds of love with the tower chimes; to Marge Williams, Jessie Hey, Pat Johnson, Barbara Minster, Sheila Crofut, Sharon Torno, and others for the wonderful desserts which so delightfully encouraged people to linger and talk; to all of you for inviting the larger community to participate in the service; to all of you who came, and all of you who wanted to come but could not, yet kept us in your prayers; to Pastor Judith for conceiving the idea of Peter's Tree and caring for the idea until it happened; and for Judith's sensitive, compassionate, warm, and wise words of comfort and hope.

A year ago you invited us to the same place for a grand celebration of a ten-year pastorate among you. That event was the last time Peter visited Eagle Harbor Church. How marvelous it was to gather together again for such a beautiful expression of your care for us.

We love you all. Thank you.

Sincerely,

Lynnea and Don and the Mayer Family

Shoes to Fill

July 10, on the ferry

Dear Peter,

It's been almost a month since I've written. I've gradually become more accustomed to the presence of your absence, and so I am less compelled to put thoughts on paper. The mental correspondence, however, continues intermittently and frequently.

I don't shake my head in disbelief so much as I did. I find I do clench my teeth whenever I happen to think of the sudden simple bang on your head that killed you.

I don't like the idea of getting accustomed to your forever absence. You are too irreplaceable. I want to continue to be keenly aware of all that makes you that way. All that makes you you.

I thought of what makes a person him- or herself when I turned down a job offer today. The director of the Horizon House Retirement Home resigned. I've been a member of the Board there, and today the Board offered me the position of Interim Director. I said "No" because I need to get ready for teaching United Church of Christ history and polity at the School of Theology and Ministry at Seattle University. But I also think it would not have been the job for me.

On the other hand, it probably would have been a job for you—not that you would have been interested. But Mom and I had heard for a long time about your natural gifts in dealing with customers (you would have been great with residents), and with team building, supportive staff relationships, not to mention your understanding of financial management.

Those positive "rumors" about your work were confirmed when after your death Compass Bank gave us a copy of the "Executive Appraisal" which was confidential appraisal of your "psychological resources." About you, it said:

"He quietly develops a network of contacts . . . seeks favorable social environments where he can continue to develop and maintain relationships . . . His optimistic attitude will have a favorable effect on those around him . . . he is willing to accept others . . . outgoing . . . a consensus builder . . . calm, even-keeled approach . . . will build cooperative relationships . . . delegate work . . . keep bigger picture considerations in mind . . ."

Your Mom and I were impressed, Pete!

As you know, I wear your dress shoes once in a while. They are just a little large for me. It figures. When I think of your warmly positive approach to problems (and problem people), your good humor—all that good soul in you is a little larger than mine, I think.

How odd. It is not uncommon for offspring to emulate the character of a deceased parent. But odd for a dad to emulate the character of a deceased son! But I want to do that, Pete. Maybe this continuing dialogue with you will soften some of my self-righteous edges, and keep me from getting sour. Maybe that begins with me being a little sweeter to myself; right, Pete?

Linda seems to continue to grieve well. It seems fortunate to me that she was never dependent on you for decision making. She has handled a lot of big ones since you died, especially the purchase of the house for herself and Chelsey.

Chelsey is just great fun—a wonderfully imaginative tease and ready to be a friend to anyone. In both those ways, Chelsey seems to be growing into your shoes quite nicely, Peter.
Love, Dad

Keeping in Touch, Letting Go

August 7, at home, Bainbridge

Dear Peter,

It's been more than a month since I last wrote to you. But as you surely know, I think about you every day and usually several times each day, usually when there's something I want to share with you, or something that reminds me of you. Mom does the same thing.

That strange mix of goodness and grief continues. This year has been a remarkably wonderful year in spite of your death. Mom and I are enjoying one event after another, which is just the kinds of thing we want to do. But everything has that other dimension: the fact that you are dead. So often in our most joy-filled moments we want to cry. And sometimes we do.

Last week was typical. We had a marvelous time with our friends John and Karen on their boat up on Desolation Sound, British Columbia. Gorgeous scenery, splendid weather, wonderful food, swimming in those surprisingly warm waters, fine company. Our kayak made a great dingy for their 44-foot Grand Banks. You would have loved it! Topside in swimsuits 10:30 at night. Making love in our snug forward cabin . . .

We talked about you. A lot. And explaining that we can only really enjoy such a time if we can make the faith assumption that you are somehow enjoying our joy. I don't think I could laugh at anything if I did not think you were laughing with me. Well, maybe that statement is a little too exclusive. I suppose that God can bring a sense of abundant life for those who grieve even if they do not believe in "life after death," as it is called. Or even believe in God, for that matter. But we choose to believe—and thereby our life has a richness and depth that I think would not be true otherwise.

I'm home on Bainbridge, out on your deck, as I write. Your presence is so much here. On Mother's Day a couple of years ago when somebody put their foot through the old deck, you convinced us it was time to build a new one!

Your design. Your work with Joe, whom we hired to be contractor. I find myself wondering which nails you pounded. The solidity of the deck is a memento of the solidity of your presence then in those four remarkably rain-free days before the Thanksgiving weekend. We pounded in the last few nails just as it began to rain.

There is a lot of you here, Pete. The wine rack, the bent wood plant hanger, the yard lights, the benches on the deck, the hammock, the tire swing. How is it that you always gave us something we all could enjoy at home? Linda continues the practice—the garden bench, the garden whimsy, yard candles . . .

Like I said, and as you probably know, it has been a wonderful summer. The backpack that Mom and I did—first time in years she could hike that much without knee pain, thanks to her diligent work with physical therapy. We talked about you at night—sipping apricot brandy in the glow of the candle lantern. Lovely time, beautiful. We cried.

We continue to get notes of comfort. You remember that Mom was a Mary Kay representative for the last ten years. Consultants all around the country sent notes to Mom. Mary Kay's personal representative wrote about Mary Kay's loss of a daughter. I held Mom while she cried.

We celebrated Tim's 40th birthday. A fine party on the deck of their house in Portland. But we talked about how, somehow even from Birmingham, you would have made us observe the day with something outrageous, raucous, and hilarious.

Hannah loves the video of *Mary Poppins*. Remember the scene where characters laugh as they float up to the ceiling? When she hears the actor Ed Wynn's laugh, Hannah says, "It's Uncle Pete!" She's right—sounds just like your laugh sometimes.

I got a new computer. Stuck on the old one was a note with your Birmingham e-mail address. I never got a chance to use it. I hated to throw it away.

You remember the Feldts, our next-door neighbors in St. Louis for fourteen years? Kathy, same age as Sarah, wrote asking us, Tim, Sarah, and you, for stories about her sister Marie, celebrating Marie's 40th birthday. I wonder what you would have written. In the years when you were 5, 6, or 7 you were often designated "Peter the Pirate" by your brother and the Feldt kids, who enticed you to chase them around the yard with your cardboard sword. They sometimes took refuge in the piano box fort.

How odd it is that Dad Feldt died suddenly of a stroke, also at age 38. We were next door to their grief for a long time—but eventually they again became the life-loving family we knew before. I wrote Kathy our sad news about you.

Pat Boesch wrote a beautiful note. You probably remember that family from the church in DeKalb. Her first husband died of cancer just after we moved there, a loss to the whole farm community. She is very happily married again. But it was a long, hard time for her.

Pat taught me something I did not expect about grieving. She became depressed several months after Earl's death when she realized the pain of losing him was becoming less intense. She said she felt that losing the pain was like losing her last intense feeling of love for Earl.

Maybe that's why I want to write to you all the time. It's a way of keeping in touch, without actually being able to touch. But I think there will also be a time of letting go, with gentle help from our faithful God.

The section of the book of Isaiah that begins in chapter 40 is filled with wise comfort for a people who have experienced terrible loss. I can't remember when I underlined 43:18–19, which says:

"Remember not the former things,
    nor consider things of old.
Behold, I am doing a new thing;
    now it springs forth, do you not perceive it?"
(RSV)

In the margin by those lines I wrote, "Get this!" It was so long ago that I have no idea what made those lines so pertinent then, but they do seem pertinent now. Not that any of us are going to give up the enjoyment of remembering you, Pete! But we will not always want to stay in that mode. We will try to continue to perceive the new life which God promises.

Well, I need to get ready for a wedding rehearsal. I felt kind of down all day. But now I feel better, and I think that's because I took the time to write out all the muddled stuff about you, and to sense again the touch of a healing Spirit.
Love, Dad

Again, The Presence of Your Absence

August 13, on the ferry, topside

Dear Peter,

My God, the view from here is simply gorgeous!
Olympics and Cascades shimmering, sailboats every-
where on the Sound . . . if you were in Birmingham I'd
be e-mailing you marine weather reports trying to has-
ten the day when you brought your boat and your family back to the Northwest. I don't know if climate and
topography would have offset that six-figure salary you
were so excited about, but we'd have worked at it!

The strangeness of this year continues, Peter. If it
were not for your death, this year would be uninterrupted seasons of blessedness. I cannot remember a time so
stress-free and so filled with what Mom and I most enjoy doing—hiking, kayaking, theatre, supper on the deck
with friends, badminton, fun with grandkids, the excitement of developing a new kind of theological school
unique and unprecedented, and enjoying our growing
connections with Plymouth Church. All that good stuff!

Yet, as I have observed previously, some of the
best times are also those times when we miss you most.
Like the wedding at which I officiated last Saturday evening up at Manor Farm—lovable couple, good friends
Barbara and Stephen among the guests, great reception
time, elegant dinner—including a superb home-brew
you would have loved! Full moon, string trio playing
fine classical pieces, then a seven piece jazz-band—an
invitation to dance which even I could not resist!

But somehow I was suddenly hit in the stomach
with your irrevocable unending deadness. It doubled me
over. For the first time in weeks, those convulsive sobs.
Mom held me, Barbara too. It only lasted a few minutes.
Then we danced again. Something about the beauty of
the evening tapped into that lingering pool of sadness,

usually overlaid with the unrelenting blessings of this
year.

I miss you, Pete. We miss you. Just before the sobs
began—and while sobbing—I clenched my teeth and
squeezed my eyes shut. I still don't want to take in the
reality of your death, Peter—your unending ever-present
absence. If it were not for the fact that I choose to believe that somehow, by the grace of a loving, life-giving
God, in a way far beyond my capacity to understand
or imagine, you are still you, you are aware of and responding to these letters, aware of and responding to
all that is happening with us, I could not enjoy any of it.
Your deadness would flatten everything. But I choose to
believe in a reality that is labeled God's power of resurrection. I believe the reality of what I have preached in
hundreds of memorial services: that among other ways,
God's comfort comes through our trust that you are
resurrected into the presence of your Loving Creator,
through whom we are also raised from the darkness of
grieving to life which has in it brightness and beauty,
gladness and joy once more.

That is happening, Peter, and we receive it gladly,
even when it is mixed with the sharp sudden painful
presence of your absence.
Love, Dad

Beauty and Broken

August 25, Bainbridge

Dear Peter,

It's that paradoxical time again—the combination of incredible beauty and blessedness along with the continuing presence of your absence.

Life is punctuated with repeated reminders of you. Like last night on the deck (the deck you built) with friends, our neighbor's dog paid us an exuberant visit, her tail whacking a wine glass, shattering one from the set you and Linda gave us.

Last week your brother Tim and I did a great backpacking trip in the Eagle Cap Wilderness. Magnificent! We thought of you a lot, sometimes out loud, often privately. Tim says he thinks of you all the time, especially when he is alone. Me too. Yet Tim also says it is so hard to believe you are actually dead.

The days with Tim were a real treat. But I think it was a time more subdued than it might have been—certainly more subdued than if you had been with us! We talked about how if you were in Birmingham now, we would have been recording comments and observations about the beauty of the hike, as part of a continuing campaign to get you to move back to the Northwest as soon as possible. As it was we merely talked about how we would have done that.

You were a multiplier factor in the family, Pete. We lost not only you but your effect on each of us, each of our reactions to you, and each person's reactions to those reactions, our responses to each other's responses to you.

All that is different now. When the family is together, it is quieter than when you were with us. We are still trying to reconnect all those broken strands between each and all of us and you. But like the wine glass, some things can't be glued together. Lots of stuff broke and was lost forever when you got whacked in the head, Pete.

I still don't want to accept your death. In a sort of silly way sometimes I feel like saying, "Peter! Dying was such a dumb thing to do. You should have checked with us first!"

For Linda and Chelsey there must be enormous pain in the paradox of simultaneous good times and grief times. Just a couple of weeks ago, they joined all your good friends on the houseboat on Lake Shasta, your regular summertime relaxed adventure. Linda reported that after a while on the boat, suddenly Chelsey began to cry, sobbing for an hour, "Why can't God bring my daddy back?"

Yet Chelsey is also that outgoing, happy, teasing (as was the practice of her daddy) five-and-a-half-year-old. For your brother-in-law Jim, Chelsey was demonstrating her ability to make Donald Duck noises by squeezing her hands together. Jim was impressed. "Who taught you to do that, Chelsey?"

"My Daddy," she replied proudly.

Chelsey had such a wonderful beginning with you and Linda, Peter. We are glad for that. We wish you had not left so soon.

Love, Dad

The Flight Not Taken

August 31, in flight to St. Louis

Dear Peter,

As you know, presumably, Mom and I are on a flight
something like the one that we had planned back in
April, before you were killed. Or, to put it another way,
it is the flight we would have taken to Birmingham at
this time to visit you and Chelsey and Linda in your new
home. We figured that by this time you'd be well settled
there, but still eager to show us your discoveries. We'd
have seen where Chelsey would be going to school. We'd
have enjoyed cruising new waters in your boat. We'd
have visited that brew pub you found, and noted the lack
of fine Northwest microbrews. We would have . . . you
can finish the sentences, Pete.

Instead, we are on our way to visit dear friends in
St. Louis, seeing once again the places you enjoyed so
much growing up, and appreciating again why your jazz-
musician brother played, "Summertime" and "St. Louie
Blues" at your memorial service.

The other day I was poking in my files to find
copies of the first of these letters to you, and I came
across your first e-mail to me about the job offer in
Birmingham: ". . . a $45,000 increase in salary." Mom
heard me moan when I found it.

There are only a few such tangible reminders of
your last months among us. I still can't throw away the
note with your Birmingham mailing address on it.

I wore your shoes again for the wedding for our
friends, the Penningtons. The setting was their multi-
level deck overlooking Fletcher Bay. Elegant! Sarah was
up visiting for the weekend and she came along.

Yesterday, Mom reached into the cupboard for the
mug with Sarah's name on it. The one she grabbed had
your name on it. Tears again.

Love, Dad

Summertime and St. Louie Blues

Sept. 10, 1998, after the trip to St. Louis, back home

Dear Peter,

As you know, we had a fine time in St. Louis! We did
so many things you would have loved. As I said to our
friends Pienings and Ellerbrakes, if there is any way that
you are participating in experience through us, you had
a ball!

We enjoyed Ted Drews Frozen Custard! Right there
on old Rt. 66, a half block from where we lived, where
you got your first job. They still do a gold rush business.
Ellerbrakes had never been there. They loved it!

We saw what had been our parsonage home, the
magnolia tree you kids planted one Mother's Day now
huge! We think we may plant a magnolia for you, Pete, if
we can find a spot in our yard with sufficient sunshine.
Our former backyard in St. Louis looks like a postage
stamp compared to our site out here. We look forward
to the time when we can take Chelsey back to St. Louis,
when we can say, "Here is where your daddy . . .'; "We
remember when your daddy . . ."

The splendid overnight at Lynne and Bob's farm on
the edge of the Ozarks included the best Missouri summertime stuff—swimming and catching bass in Indian
Creek, with the temperature a muggy 99 degrees—perfect for sipping gin and tonic on their deck, serenaded
by the twilling singing of cicadas. It was from their farm
that Lynne and Bob sent soil to be added to the planting of the cherry tree in your memory at Eagle Harbor
Church.

We visited with the folks so important to us and
to you in your growing up years—Dippels, Lindberghs,
and others.

It was a fine reunion with Ellerbrakes—Dick, my
roommate in college, inspiration for my trip around the

world, best man at each other's weddings. Johann wore your Mom's wedding dress. We often visited their farm place when you kids were growing up. You may remember David, same age as you, killed in an auto accident when he was twenty-two. When we got the bad news, we immediately drove three hundred miles to be with them. It was our first close encounter with such stupendous loss.

When you were killed, Richard said, "From our beginnings together I knew we would always be bonded, Donald—but I never thought we would be bonded like this."

After Richard's mom heard about your death, she sent us a note: "When my grandson, David was killed, for reasons I do not understand, I could not cry. Since I learned of Peter's death, the tears have not stopped flowing."

Caught bluegills in Ellerbrakes' big farm pond, and remembered that time we camped with Ellerbrakes at Roaring Springs State Park at the beginning of trout season. You were about four. It was cold and rainy—the rest of us were miserable by the end of the day. But you walked back to our sputtering campfire beaming with delight, carrying a huge sucker that some disgusted fisherman had given you. It was the highlight of the day!

I wonder if you and David have encountered each other. How is it there, Peter? Where is 'there'?

In our visits, we talked a lot about loss, death, memories. And about faith. With tears, sometimes.

We love you so much, Peter. Sometimes I find myself saying, "We loved you." But I reject the past tense!

It's odd—I took along the videotape of your memorial service. But we didn't play it. I wonder if we will. Ever?

I think I'd like to—so that our friends who were not there can hear those astonishing testimonies about you. And so that we can hear them again too. I am a little shy about imposing it on others. I don't know why.

When I unpacked from our trip to St. Louis I picked up that video from where it was buried in the luggage. It is labeled "Peter Karl." When I first saw it, it seemed for an instant that it was something you had accidentally left with us and I needed to return it to you.

So I still resist your death, Peter. The ever-present finality of your absence.

Love, Dad

A Time to Embrace

September 13, 6:15 p.m., on the ferry

Dear Peter,

We were close for a moment yesterday, right? You know what I mean. Mom and I in worship at Plymouth Church. Marvelous liturgy, music. It happened during the second verse of the second hymn—I can't remember the words—I was caught by your presence and your absence at the same time. It was a moment when the reality of both was porous.

Of course, it hit me in the stomach again and my tears flowed. I stifled the sobs. I did not want to call attention to myself. Not even Mom noticed. But we were together. You and me and Mom, for a moment. There was an unbelievable (but I choose to believe in it) warmth, a profound sense of God's love enfolding all of us. And again a deep sense that you are more than okay.

But God, we miss you, Peter. I still find myself now and then clenching my teeth, shaking my head, not wanting to take in your death. It is so painfully easy to imagine a hundred different scenarios in which you would simply still be alive.

This afternoon one of my colleagues at the School of Theology and Ministry told me that he has had difficulty communicating with his son, who happens to be your age. Your death, he said, has pushed him to try harder, realizing that if his son had died as you have died, there would be much left unresolved between them.

I certainly do not feel that way about you and me, Peter. No regrets. I just miss you.

During our visit back in St. Louis, we talked with longtime friends whose son is your age. Twenty years ago, an accident left him near death for a long time, and since then a quadriplegic, alive only with a respirator, nourished though a tube in his stomach. Recently their son is experiencing pain once again, with increasing intensity, and no relief seems possible. With deep sadness his mom said, "Sometimes I wonder if we made the right decision."

I am thankful—I guess—that we were not compelled to make a decision about whether you should live or die. But I would have liked to have had a chance to join in a fight for your life. I think. Who knows? As it is, we trust that you are now more than okay. And that helps Mom and me to enjoy the abundant gift of each day.

It must be yesterday's moment which enables me to feel especially close to you today.
Love, Dad

The Hardest Annual Letter

Lynnea and Don Mayer—Bainbridge Island, WA. 98110

Thanksgiving, 1998
Dear Ones,
This is the hardest annual letter we've ever tried to write.
For in it we must tell you of our terrible loss and deep
grief. Most, but not all of you know, that our son Peter
was killed in a one-car accident on the night of April
5. We gathered for the memorial service for Peter at
Hillsdale Church in Portland the day before Easter. On
Palm Sunday, the day Peter was killed, Lynnea and I
had worshiped at Plymouth Church in Seattle, and then
had lunch with Tony Robinson, the pastor, and his wife,
Linda. We had been deeply moved by Tony's sermon and
prayer speaking of how often we go through our own
Holy Week experiences. Sometime after midnight, Tim's
call came and a world ended.

Peter and Linda would have celebrated their 10th
wedding anniversary April 29. He would have been 38
on May 15.

Good friends and former banking associates
had recruited Peter to a senior-level position with the
Compass Bank in Birmingham, Alabama. At the end of
January, we'd all gathered for a warm and wonderful ski
weekend at Sun River, Oregon, just before Peter began
working in Birmingham. Linda and Chelsey went with
Peter where they bought a new home and planned its
décor. Linda and Chelsey returned to sell their home in
Portland and get ready to move to Birmingham around
the middle of April. Peter kept everybody at work
informed about exactly how many days he had been
separated from Linda and Chelsey and how many days
before they would be reunited.

Lynnea and I were enjoying all that retirement folks
say they enjoy: more time with our five grandchildren,

and with friends; theatre; music; art; hikes; kayaking. I enjoyed the thrill (and terror) of singing the tenor solos for three performances of Beethoven's *Mass in C*, with a ninety-voice chorale and full symphony. Linda and Chelsey came up for the last performance, a week before Peter was killed.

A son was born to Sarah and Jim on March 14th, with Hannah now big sister. They named him Peter Philip Skutt. He's great with grins and chuckles. They too had purchased a new home. The family housewarming was also to be the farewell party for Peter and Linda and Chelsey, April 12.

Tim and Sue have also made a beautiful addition to their home, adding a bedroom and bath, and more space for Miles and Erin. They had a great vacation in Death Valley and Nevada in March just before Sue went back to work from her maternity leave.

In June we made a wonderful trip to California with Linda and Chelsey, visiting Carl and Wilma, (Chelsey riding Carl's quarter horse, Spinit, and tripling his ration of carrots). We visited Lynnea's step-mom, Kay, and her half-brother, Karl, with Disneyland, Sea World, etc., on our happy tourist itinerary.

Linda is a great Mom, and a person of courageous decisiveness. She bought a fine new house in suburban Portland in a neighborhood with lots of playmates for Chelsey. Chelsey catches the school bus to kindergarten. ("We get to do homework!") She talks about her Daddy often, sometimes with great enthusiasm, sometimes with tears.

In August, Tim and Don did a splendid backpack in the Wallowa Mountains, Eagle Cap Wilderness in eastern Oregon. We kayaked to Blake Island one Sunday for lunch, dodging both the ferry and an aircraft carrier.

We had planned to spend the week after Easter in St. Louis for the Eden Theological Seminary reunion. Instead we used the tickets in September, celebrating our 42nd wedding anniversary with good visits to family and friends.

In one of those coincidences which make one think again about Providence, a few days after Peter's death, we got an e-mail from Perth, Australia: "Greetings! You are probably wondering who this is." The who turned out to be Lynnea's second cousin, Chris Roberts and her husband, Frank, sent our way on business for the U. of Western Australia. We'd never met or even corresponded before. It was cousin love at first sight! We're heading for Perth in February. And, in keeping with the go-go stage of retirement we will tour Morocco with the Ellerbrakes in January.

Late in September, Dad Mayer stopped eating. With our children and grandchildren we gathered for a simple communion service on a Sunday afternoon. Dad joined us in singing, "Blesed be the ties that bind . . ." and "What a friend . . ." and "Shall we gather at the river . . ." He touched his five great-grandchildren. "Oh, I have a wonderful family!"

He died the following Thursday, Sept. 24, the same day I started teaching UCC History and Polity at the School of Theology and Ministry at Seattle. He would have been so proud of the UCC involvement in this bold new ecumenical venture. It was a deeply moving passing of the torch. Our memorial service for Dad was also at Hillsdale Church, Sept. 27.

So here we are. Approaching the holidays in a world without Peter and Dad. One way of talking about how it is with us is to say that we think each of us is grieving well. Dad's death was about as good and timely as anyone might expect. He was 92.

We are open to the pain of Peter's death, and pour it out in our own times and ways. And we are open to the comfort. We are comforted by persons like yourselves, far more tenderly, thoughtfully, and abundantly than we could ever have imagined.

Part of the comfort came through memorial gifts from all over now totaling thousands of dollars for Habitat for Humanity in which Peter was much involved.

Lots of our comfort has come through our faith and the faith community near and far. Our faithful black lab, Yoshi, now an 11½-year-old puppy, persistently engages us in play. So we have been released for laughter and loving, perceiving blessings, finding sweetness and bright beauty, sharply defined always in the shadowing sadness of life without Peter. It may be harder for Tim and Sarah than it is for us simply because their circle of friends is less acquainted with how long grief continues to work its ways.

So we will gather at Sarah's house for Thanksgiving. Sarah, Jim, Hannah 3 1/2, Peter 8 months; Tim, Sue, Miles (nearly 5), and Erin (almost a year old). Linda and Chelsey will host Linda's family at her house on Thanksgiving Day, and we'll gather with her and Chelsey later on that weekend.

Thank you all so much for all your loving care. We look forward to hearing from you. We love you. We keep you in our prayers.

Lynnea and Don
Linda Lacey and Chelsey Mayer
Susan Powers and Tim Mayer
Sarah and Jim Skutt

Far More Than We Are Able to Imagine

December 14, 1998—9 a.m.

Dear Peter,
The auto decks of the 8:45 ferry filled early—so Mom is a walk-on for her M.D. appointment, and I'll sit here in the parking lot waiting for the next ferry.

As you know, it's been a long time since I've written. There have certainly been lots of times when I have wanted to write. And yet, I can't remember the last time I actually did.

I think all of the family thinks about you all the time. In each of us there is that pool of grief. I still feel your loss most in very good times. Last week at the Wednesday noontime jazz worship—the prelude so beautiful—I was sitting by myself off to the side, so I gave myself permission to cry, my stomach pumping out the tears from the pool of grief each of us carries inside us.

There are many times when my tears might come easily, but I do not want to call attention to myself. We are singing the *Charlie Brown Christmas* piece in the Bainbridge Chorale. Of course that music does it! You played the Charlie Brown themes so often—almost all that remained of your years of piano lessons, so abruptly ended twenty years ago with your motorcycle accident.

But I get through such moments—no, better to say, I am free to fully enjoy good times with Mom, family, friends, because I trust that you are present with us, enjoying the time with us. I visualize you doing so, cheering us on, offering counsel and encouragement.

It is necessary to believe that at the same time you are with Mom and me, you can be and are also present with Linda and Chelsey, and everybody else who loved you—because I would not want to call you away from them.

Sometimes I imagine that your grandparents and other family are also with you and with us. Such imaginings are a stretch—imagining an unimaginable reality— but a comfort in the face of such unbearable loss. Such imagining is grounded in my trust in the faithfulness of God to each of us, and my trust in God's ability to do "far more than we dare to ask or even imagine." I'm convinced God created us to live and grow through loving relationships, so why not believe that God continues to value each of us and our relationships beyond the limits of this earthly existence?

I'll go along with Paul, convinced that "nothing in life nor death is able to separate us from the love of God as we know it in Christ Jesus" (Romans 8:38–39). Or I play on the comment on parenting from Jesus in Matthew 7:7–11 to the effect that if we know how to give good things to our children, how much more is God able to provide? Just so, if we converted half our garage into a bunk room to accommodate Chelsey and her cousins, how much more has God in heaven provided abundant lodging (John 14:2).

Of course you know, Peter, I write these letters for my benefit rather than yours—since with Paul in his First letter to the Corinthians, chapter 13, I presume that now you already know and "understand fully" just as you, and we, "have been fully understood" (v. 13, RSV). I think Paul also got in it right in the same paragraph in that letter where he says that "now we see as though we were looking into a dark mirror." My imagination of your life now is almost necessarily a mirror image of life as we know it on this side of death—actually it may be both very much like and unlike life here. "Then," as Paul says, "we shall see face to face."

I choose to think that at a minimum, life now for you and others with God is an existence that continues to value persons, all persons, now fully healed and fully graced with forgiveness and love. It is the grace factor which enables me to anticipate enjoying the company there of people that I can't stand here!

Sometimes I am impatient with my pictures of life after death, because in comparison with the drama, beauty, and challenge of life on this side of death, my somewhat traditional imaginings are pretty boring! I like to take naps, but the notion of eternal rest does not fill me with enthusiasm!

Love, Dad

Advent Encouragement

December 14, 1998

Dear Peter,

As you know, your sister, Sarah, continues to have a hard time with your death. Having given birth to their Peter just a month before you were killed, it has been impossible for her to fully rejoice in that birth and at the same time fully grieve your death. She simply has not had the time or the solitude to deal with all that, and still be a wife to Jim and a mom to young Hannah, as well as little Peter.

Nor has she had many listeners to the expressions of her grief. People your age, Pete, thirty- or forty-something, are not so likely to be "acquainted with grief," and naturally do not want to be. Our friend Barbara calls them "virgin grievers." As I observed previously, for the most part, the persons in Sarah and Jim's circle of friends do not understand how long grief wants to have its way with us. Mom and I are blessed with a much more understanding community, gifted with a patience grounded in empathy and compassion.

But you know, Pete, one thing about your death that still gives me trouble is the recognition of just how casually you got yourself killed. That sense of casualness bleeds into our memory of times when we had hoped you'd join us at some simple family event—but you had something else on your agenda.

Some weeks ago, you may remember, I was standing at the sink with Linda helping with dishes, and I began to say something like, "Sometimes I wish . . ." At that moment Linda teared and said, "Yes, I wish someone had made some different choices, mainly him!" Meaning you, of course, Pete.

That abrupt fall from our high time together to the reality of you suddenly dropping out is still hard to take in. It was so simple for you to get killed, so easy. A snap, one might say. We're still a little ticked off about that.

Barbara would like me to do some sessions on grief for Bethany Lutheran Church sometime next spring. It happens that one might be scheduled for Palm Sunday. Wouldn't that be a powerful time—an opportunity to talk about how often many of us go through our personal Holy Week—just as was preached to us in the sermon the morning before we learned of your death.

We love you, Peter. Sometimes when I really need it, I feel your love cheering me on. We'll need you, Pete, when we hang that old silver ornament on the Christmas tree, the one with your name on it.

Love, Dad

Always One Is Missing

Monday, March 8, 1999

Dear Peter,

As you know, it's been three months since I last wrote to you. In part, that is because I feel I have little new to say. My grief no longer produces those convulsive sobs, but now takes the form of a nearly ever-present sadness, a repeated disappointment, a simple wish you had not been killed. Sometimes your absence feels like you simply decided not to join us for a family event. I then feel disappointed, like you have let us down.

Yesterday, as you know, was one of those big family days—baptisms for Erin and Peter, plus Susan's fortieth birthday. And that odd feeling happened again, when we gathered for a family photo in front of the church after worship: Tim, Sue, Miles, Erin; and Mom and me; and Sarah, Jim, Hannah, Peter; and Linda and Chelsey. I found myself half consciously waiting for the rest of the family to join us; then I realized it was you that I was waiting for.

Yes, it always feels like part of the family is missing. I think, Peter, that my reaction is evidence of what I have called your multiplier effect among us. What we miss is not simply your presence, but what your presence created among us—all the interactions that you produced among us. Now there is only the presence of your absence, a void, a silence, an emptiness that hangs around the edges of our gatherings. My half-conscious reaction is not, "Peter, we miss you," but rather, "Hey, Pete, where are you?"

Susan wanted a quiet 40th birthday, and Tim complied. It was a fine celebration, not much teasing about it being the 40th, but it is not hard to imagine how the whole atmosphere would have been hilariously different had you been there.

And, Peter, you know that yesterday was a hard day for Linda. All the rest of us have our spouses in our grieving; she has only Chelsey. And it is Linda who has the day-by-day, minute-by-minute reminders of your absence, especially now as we approach the first anniversary of your death.

Sarah thinks it is especially hard for Linda because you had grown so much in your relationship with each other and were so eager for more. Mom and I will never forget the night you invited the two of us over to join the two of you in your hot tub. That was fun in itself but—surprise!—you popped a bottle of champagne to celebrate the successful completion of weeks of counseling in your marriage! We had worried that you two were going to separate. And now, as Sarah says, "This is the ultimate separation. Linda must feel some anger about that."

Yes, and Linda must be reliving last year at this time—those last weeks of high expectations of an entirely new future with you—only to have all that future ejected from her life when you were ejected from your car.

We want to get together for the weekend of the anniversary of your death. It will be Easter, and Mom has invited everybody up. Linda is not sure. I guess she is torn between being with us, or being with some of her close friends and family in Portland. Or maybe she is not sure she wants to be with anybody. I am thinking that maybe it would be good for Linda if she and Chelsey did a kind of open house for friends and family, people dropping in to visit for a while, talking about you and life without you. I don't know if that will happen—but we will not want to be apart from Linda during that week.

Tim and Susan are talking about their future and a possible move to Hood River. Their conversation produces in me a nostalgia for those couple of years when all three families—you and Linda, Jim and Sarah, and Tim and Sue–lived within walking distance of each other. We were so privileged for so long. A move for Tim and Sue seems like a further scattering.

I am aware of how everybody's life is moving on. Sue's birthday, the baptisms, our travels, their possible move. But for us, you are mostly stuck in that time just before your 38th birthday. I am sad whenever I think of the future without you, Peter. I am especially sad whenever something wonderful is happening and you are not part of it, and we can't tell you about it.

Life is still good—so much to love, and enjoy and work for and laugh about. Life is still rich and good, and continues to be so in unexpected, unimagined ways. But we miss you, Pete—and it feels as if all that goodness and richness of life would be multiplied for us if you were still here.

Love, Dad

Understated

March 24, 1999, 4 p.m., on the ferry

Dear Peter,
As you can see, I'm up in the "library" of the ferry, top-deck, enclosed. For some reason everyone is quiet up here. No conversation and no cell phones, just fine views and a fine place to read or write. I am pushing myself to write, in spite of the reading I need to finish before my book group tomorrow night. There are always distractions from this writing task. And as I just said to Phyllis Anderson at the School of Theology and Ministry, my responses to your death are slowly changing. No longer am I so compelled to write to you.

Phyllis was right on target when she said that in a way I am losing you again. With the loss of the sharp immediacy of your death, there is that strange second grief—the grief of the loss of grief—that Pat B. talked about years ago.

But at times the sharp pain happens. It continues to happen in times of deep beauty and joy, often with music and worship, such as at the beginning of the noon jazz service today. The trio played "God of the Sparrow, God of the Whale." Such soaring beauty calls to all that is in me. And in me is your death, the heavy emptiness of your absence. And for a few moments that reality was as full as it was in the beginning—the brilliant, ripping pain of you torn out of our lives forever.

At lunch, after we had ordered the Cobb salads, Phyllis asked, "How are you?"

"Okay," I said brightly—then recognized immediately what she was really asking. I juggled the option for a bit—to talk or not talk about how I am doing after nearly a year without you.

I chose to talk. She listened. She is a good pastor and a good friend.

I talked about the session at Bethany Church last Sunday when for the first time I read a few of these letters publicly. I know—and yet I was surprised by—the power of grief among us, how it is always present among us. And how much people appreciate an implied permission to talk about their grief, and, yes, sometimes express with tears the pain still present from a long-ago loss.

And, I told Phyllis about using the chainsaw to clear the blackberry thicket where we hope to plant a magnolia in your memory, the same blackberry thicket you helped begin to clear when we first moved here eleven years ago. You'd have been right in there with the current project, Pete, sharing a beer with me afterwards.

I told Phyllis about Chelsey's excited call to us to report losing her first tooth! What you would have done with that event!

As you know, Linda decided to go ahead and plan an open house on the Saturday before Easter. We're glad she is doing it—particularly because your memorial service was on a Saturday before Easter. The invitation says, "Come by and see where Chelsey and I are living now. Give us a hug!"

Yes, yes, lots of hugs! An invitation, a permission, an excuse, for those who have been shy about connecting with those who grieve to reconnect.

As you know, Linda is a wise and courageous woman. We are amazed by all the challenges she has met since you were killed. We told her that. She said, "I'd gladly give up all that . . ." She didn't finish the sentence. She didn't need to.

We love Linda. We miss you. Both understatements.

Love, Dad

Pain, Slowly Lifting

April 9, 1999, on the ferry

Dear Peter,

Ok, I've got a few minutes to tune in with you. How is it with you, Pete?

I find I have exhausted my imagination—or, to say it another way, I've reached the limits of my imagination about what life is like for you now. Is there a "now" for you, Peter? What do you do? Is there any "doing"? I wonder as I wander . . .

Your widow, Linda, is a wonder, as you know. She has transformed their house with new furniture. Sometimes I forget that you never lived in that house— but until recently she still had your old college-age, bargain-priced purple stuffed chairs. They were one of the mementos of you that we were glad to see go!

And Linda did a marvelous thing for the anniversary week of your death. She invited everybody she could of your friends and relations to an open house the Saturday before Easter. A whole bunch came! People I'd not seen since your memorial service a year ago.

We didn't talk about you as much as I would have liked. But Linda passed out notepaper on which to write short messages to you. Late in the afternoon we gathered on the front sidewalk, attached each note to a helium balloon, and let them go.

It was quite a moment. The boisterous bunch gradually hushed as we watched the balloons go up and up and out until finally they were tiny specks disappearing into the clouds. It seemed a metaphor for the way the fresh pain of your death is fading.

Linda has now involved Chelsey in the Dougy Center, where she meets twice a month with other kids who have lost a parent. It's a good move. Linda meets with the surviving parents at the same time.

Coming across the Columbia River on the way home, Mom's eyes filled with tears. "I always think of Peter here," she said, "and how much he loved cruising these waters with Linda and Chelsey." She's right. It seems like in the last couple of years we enjoyed more of family time on that boat than anywhere else. I carry a vivid image of you coming alongside the boat on the Wave Runner, carrying a very happy Chelsey on your lap. I think Linda has not seen the boat for a year. Along the same lines, the big boxes of your clothes shipped back from Birmingham are still in the garage.

We want to go back to Portland for your wedding anniversary. We told Linda we'd like to take her out to dinner celebrating the time when she became part of our family eleven years ago.

"Okay," she said, "as long as we celebrate that part. No more wedding anniversaries."

We love you, Pete. Wish you were here.

Dad

Birthday #67

April 22, 1999, coming home on the ferry

Dear Peter,

Today is my birthday #67. I have mixed feelings about the day. I feel younger than I formerly thought sixty-seven would feel. (You are smiling about that, aren't you?) At the same time, sixty-seven is creeping up there . . . And there is a sadness about this #67 because you are not around to push the celebration in the particular way you would do it! Which is to say, I miss you today. Again.

I have been writing these letters to you for more than a year now. I considered making this one the last one. But I resist closing off this form of concentrating myself on you. These letters affirm my trust in your resurrected life. I feel like I am somehow participating in it.

The pool of grief is still there. I do not tap into it as often as I once did. But it is there and it is powerful. You saw what happened, I guess, when I read that note from Jane Lindberg. She wrote to say she thought of us at Easter, and of you encompassed by the love of God more abundantly than we could imagine.

And she enclosed a haiku, a bit of poetry which she said I had written at some kind of workshop at Hope Church long ago during the time I was pastor there and her husband, Dennis, was my associate.

> Lightning splits night sky
> Shatters reaching tree
> Yet loved seedlings grow.

When I read what I wrote back when you were about ten years old, the pool of tears surged upward and I whimpered and sobbed for a while. I sent the note and the haiku on to Linda.

135

Lots of people ask us how it's going, and wait for a response from us. We appreciate all those who remember that we continue to live each day in the overwhelming mystery of your death.—even on birthdays—but who party with us too!
Love, Dad

P.S. Well how 'bout that! We just spotted a California gray whale right off the entrance to Eagle Harbor. It is way too much to think that you had anything to do with it. But I'll think it anyway! Thanks for the b.d. gift, Pete! (Though realistically, chances are if you'd have been around, you'd have forgotten the date!)

The Haiku E-Mail

From an e-mail dated Sept. 29, 1999, from Jane Lindberg

Hi Don and Lynne!
Thought I'd share an experience that parallels the haiku you wrote.

The front of the sanctuary at Ivy Chapel is a huge window all the way across the altar that opens to the beauty of the natural setting behind it. Framed in the window is a beautiful towering tree with outreaching branches.

One year this gorgeous tree was struck by lightning. A main limb was 'amputated.' Sometime after that the Ellerbrakes lost their son, David. I found myself sitting in church one Sunday morning trying to make sense out of what seemed impossibly hopeless as I thought about them and what they must be feeling.

I found myself gazing at the old tree and noticed something that I had not taken in before. There, exactly at the place where the limb was 'amputated', new branches had sprung up! It amazed me—in the same way it amazed me when I read the Christmas letter from David's grandmother (whom we always call, Aunt Peggy). In it she reported that she had committed herself to volunteer work at Deaconess Hospital as a way of dealing with the loss of David, her medical intern grandson. He could no longer work with patients, but *she* could!

I am amazed by the new growth on the tree, the response of Grandmother Peggy Ellerbrake, and it amazes me as I see both of you embrace living as fully as you know how, in the face of your enormous loss.

Thanks be to God!

Three-Year Anniversary

April 9, 2001, Monday after Palm/Passion Sunday

Dear Peter,

As you know, we are into that season again. With a little flip, two words from yesterday's choir anthem said it: "Peter remembered . . ." This is a time when you are remembered by all of us, Peter.

The anniversary was of course April 5. We marked the day with an early phone call. Chelsey picked up the phone. We didn't know if she was aware of the anniversary, and we didn't want to distract her from catching the school bus. So we simply said we were thinking of her, we loved her, and we looked forward to seeing her at Eastertime.

It is hard to believe that she is eight years old already. She is so delightful to talk with on the phone—except when one gets a long pause on her end and you know she is also watching a video!

Then we talked with Linda for a few minutes. She said she was glad we called—it would move her to go ahead and cry and get it over with!

That's the way it is—one knows that at some time the tears will come. The only question is what will prompt them.

So each day as April 5 approached, I found myself thinking of you more and more, remembering especially that awful 1 a.m. phone call from your brother.

The season is shadowed. Dick Kroll called from Oregon, leaving a message saying he remembers the season for us, and how I had talked about Easter as "a shadowed joy." Others called or sent notes. We continue to welcome all the comfort offered, Peter. We still need it.

But Palm Sunday is the day of remembering for us, reliving, almost. Worship began with the round the block processional, the same way we did it on the day you were killed. When the choir was gathering, I saw Mom on the other side of the narthex. I walked over to say something about the special day. As I reached her, the pool of grief overflowed, triggering those heavy sobs for the first time in a long time.

The sobs are wordless now, probably because my words in these letters have said about as much as there is to say about your stunning death.

Mom held me, stroking my back. "Its okay, its okay, its okay. Are you all right?"

"Yes," I said, meaning that the wound is much healed but the amputation's phantom pain still remains.

Jim Halfaker, bless his heart, spotted us embracing, came over to enfold both of us, saying, "I remember this season. This is a hard time. I remember this time . . ."

These are days to remember you, Peter, and to remember all those who love you and care for us. And above all, to give thanks to God, who loves us all, and gives us life, life renewed, life resurrected. Perhaps one reason that we have come through all this, Peter, is that we never did stop giving thanks for God's abundant faithfulness.

Love, Dad

PART 2

From Lament to Sweetness

"The Ransomed of the Lord Shall Obtain Joy and Gladness"

Sept. 19, 2006—On the bus, Matera to Positano, Italy

Dear Peter,

Suddenly, I want to write to you again! I've been waiting for this. I don't know why I stopped writing months?, years?, ago. And I am not sure why I now want to write to you again. It must be because I want to share with you the deep joy of this time, these times, this year marked not so much by your death, Peter, but by celebrations of our life fifty years after your mom and I were married!

This trip to Sicily and south Italy is one of those celebrations, Peter—although I must say that your mom and I now come pretty close to celebrating every day. (We certainly give thanks for every day). I think last night was the epitome of the celebrations, an astonishing demonstration of how wonder-ful the healing your mom and I have experienced in these eight years since we were nearly shattered by your death.

We'd enjoyed a splendid day exploring Alberobello and Matera. Then we gathered with our tour mates for hors d'oeuvres and wine on the terrazzo in front of our cave room, overlooking the mysterious beauty of ancient Sassi, with its labyrinth of steep stairs leading to layers of cave homes down one side of the steep ravine and up the other. Hilarious conversations became more quiet, personal, serious, and thoughtful, while against the baroque sky the light of the setting sun slid up and off the tower of the old cathedral across the ravine, and little lights began to appear. It was all so rich and so beautiful that with a certain private touch and exchange of glance, your mom and I signaled an agreement to skip dinner (no appetite anyway after all those Italian wines, cheeses, and salamis on the terrace—you would have loved it, Peter!)

We slipped to our cave, showered, laughed uproari-
ously at the reflected images of our pornographic poses
in the full length mirror (even though we've not yet seen
Pompeii's "secret closet.") We made love with playful
freedom and long, deep gratitude.

Afterward, I lay awake for a long time, Peter, too
thrilled, too mysteriously elated, to sleep. And I realized
that I wanted, finally, to write to you again, to try to put
into words what has happened to me and to your mom
and I since last I wrote.

How it is that your mom and I are able to enjoy
such abundant life in spite of the massive loss of you.
To say we still miss you, Peter, is a huge understate-
ment, but your loss no longer shadows the glad times in
the way that it did. I think that realization contributed
to my elation that night in the Sassi cave. It was such a
thoroughly good and beautiful time—and I could not
help but remember that in those long months after your
death, in the midst of such a time I would break into
sobs, so heavy the presence of your absence

How strangely blessed are we who grieve!
Love, Dad

P.S. One more thought just came to me, Pete. You
know that hymn by Bryan Wren, entitled "Bring Many
Names"? Wren has the most real images of God I know.
And in the last verse, he says this:

> Great, living God, never fully known, joyful darkness
>   far beyond our seeing,
> Closer yet than breathing, everlasting home . . .

That gets at it, Peter: encompassing awe-filled darkness through grief-filled darkness to a joy-filled darkness
and everlasting home.

Home sometime for all of us, Peter?

Living through the Turn

Tuesday, Nov. 20, 2006, 1:30 p.m.

Dear Peter,

I'm writing while listening to a marvelous piece of music: NPR's broadcast of Paul McCartney's *Ecce Cor Meum* from Carnegie Hall last week, the U.S. premiere performance. I tell you, Pete, this music is a long way from "Sergeant Pepper's"!

I was half-listening to NPR's *Weekend Edition* last Saturday when an interview with Sir Paul caught my attention. If I got the story right, Magdalen College, Oxford, commissioned McCartney to do a major choral piece eight years ago. Halfway through composition, McCartney's first wife, Linda, died, and all his composition came to a halt. "I could simply not write, "he said. After some time, he began again with a section of music entitled "Lamentation." "I was able to write out my grief," he said.[1]

You can see, Peter, why I suddenly started paying attention. I have long thought that I have been "writing out" my grief in these letters. And I have always thought that these letters might appropriately be labeled "lamentations."

Nearly half the Psalms are called "laments," or complaints addressed to God. The psalmist sings the blues about the Cosmic Lover, laying down an elaborate gripe against God for the unfair way God is managing the universe in generally, and the psalmist's life in particular. Actually, it's a pretty healthy thing to do—being honest

1. Paul McCartney, "Sir Paul McCartney's Choral Piece." Interview by Susan Stanberg, *Weekend Edition Saturday*, hosted by Scott Simon, NPR, November 18, 2006. Online: http://www.npr .org/templates/transcript/transcript.php?storyId=6506936/.

to God. Unfortunately, Sunday-morning worship is usually too polite to include our protests!

A long time ago, Pete, I happened to learn by accident the healthfulness of lamenting from our good friend Walter Brueggemann. You remember being at Camp Mo-Val, Peter, out there in the Ozarks, sheltered in our old umbrella tent, catching big-mouth bass in the lake, hiking in among the dogwood and cedars, always on the lookout for copperheads. One summer camp week, Walter was invited out there to do his stuff on Psalms for high-school camp. I was there the same week doing a gig on voluntary service, showing my slides from Hong Kong and India.

At the time I was about two years into my tenure as associate to Rev. Z. (as he invited everybody to call him). And, as is not uncommon for associate pastors, I was mad as hell—in my case, angry at the way I saw Rev. Z. undermining my assigned work in Christian education. I was so stressed out and angry that for the first (and last) time in my life I developed hemorrhoids. Talk about a pain in the . . . !

Even though Walter was only beginning his stellar career as a biblical theologian, I already knew I could learn a lot from my former classmate. So I sat with the high-schoolers while Walter did a week's work with the Psalms. He taught us about several types of psalms, but the psalm I most remember is Psalm 35.

Something incredible happened to me as I listened to Walter explicate the ways in which that ancient, angry, anonymous singer of the blues poured out line after line of bitter complaint about the way he was being treated. The poet demanded justice, pleaded for revenge! Finally, after twenty-six verses of painful, anguished, angry honesty, there is what interpreters of the lament psalms have labeled "the turn." Abruptly the psalm turns from lament to the psalmist's expectation of restoration to well-being, a vindication so remarkable that his friends will shout for joy and praise the God "who delights in the welfare of his servant" (v. 27, RSV).

I'll always remember Walter's summary comment about the psalm: "What a petty complaint; but what a great God!" My old RSV still carries my comment scribbled under the last line of Psalm 35: "TREMENDOUS!"

With Walter's leading that afternoon, I got the message that it was very much okay to pour out my anger to God. Your mom and I sat in bed and prayed about it— one of the rare times we did that. And guess what? My hemorrhoids disappeared! (Yes, Pete, I hear you—the healing power of word, right?)

In later years, Walter did a small piece in *The Psalms of Life and Faith* about the Lament Psalms that he entitled "The Formfulness of Grief."[2] In it he notes that it is characteristic of the people of biblical faith to pour out their grievous complaint to God in the lament form, detailed with gritty, earthy candor, followed by the turn to a promise of praise for the anticipated restoration to fullness of life. In one summary line on page 96, Brueggemann writes, "Israel has, by the form, decided about loss, grief, and death. They are real and they are dangerous; but Yahweh deals with them."[3]

It is important to notice, Pete, that the turn to praise happens without any change in the outward circumstances of the lamenter. Hence, I continued to share ministry with Rev. Z. Likewise, you are still, to all outward appearances, dead. The turn to praise is entirely grounded in the trust that God is able to comfort.

I kept Walter's piece for a long time, and it is probably still buried in my files somewhere. But the memory of it, the basic thesis, has been quite helpful to me over

2. Walter Brueggemann, "The Formfulness of Grief," in *The Psalms and the Life of Faith*, ed. Patrick D. Miller (Minneapolis: Fortress, 1995) 84–97.

3. Ibid., 96.

the years, Peter, and never more so than in those first months after you were killed.

I think that your mom and I have lived through the "turn."

Love, Dad

From Lament to Sweetness

November 21, 2006, 6:35 p.m.

Dear Peter,
It is still raining! Mom and I are on the ferry heading for
choir rehearsal. We are not looking forward to hiking
up the hill in this miserably cold rain. Where is global
warming when we need it!

That question is, of course, a lament. I have been
talking about the relation between lament and healing.
You might observe that I obviously believe in that connection because over and over again in these letters I
have reported our tears and sobs!

One of my favorite biblical texts comes at the end
of Ezekiel chapter 2 and the beginning of chapter 3.
Ezekiel is called to be a pastor to the grieving people of
Israel who are languishing in exile. The call comes in a
strange vision, as follows: .

> I looked, [and] behold, a hand was stretched out to
> me, and, lo, a written scroll was in it . . .
> Written on the front and on the back . . . words of
> lamentation and mourning and woe . . . [Ezek
> 2:9–10, RSV]
> And, he said to me, . . . 'eat this scroll . . . fill your
> stomach with it.'
> Then I ate it; and in my mouth it was sweet as honey."
> [Ezek 3:1, 3, RSV]

About forty years ago I scribbled a note in the margin of that text: "Good sermons are processed through
one's stomach!" By that I have meant that the preaching
which gets into the listener's life depends on the text
having first been digested into the preacher's life. I am
convinced that claim is true. But for the last few years,
I've looked at that text from a different angle. I've taken
seriously the fact that it is a lament that Ezekiel eats.

Ezekiel takes in the grief, the pain of loss, fully, every last bite! And lo, the lament becomes sweet as honey!

That certainly cannot mean that one finds it sweet to wallow in one's grief. I think rather the text is saying that the process of healing the pain of loss begins with fully accepting the pain of loss. Ezekiel is called to minister to people in deep grief. Taking into himself the pain, facing fully the darkness in himself, opens the way for the transformative mystery of healing.

The lament psalms certainly influenced the way Mom and I expressed our grief about your death. Of course the lament psalms are addressed to God, whereas my letters are addressed to you. But I always feel that God is reading these letters over your shoulder. And I am convinced that only as we were able to express the pain of our loss, and only when we were able to pump out the grief that is in us, only then is the emptiness of life without you slowly filled with an abiding sense of well-being once again—the move from lament to praise, which is called "the turn."

In the lament psalms there is typically a fair amount of anger, or at least great impatience, directed toward God. Psalm 22:2—"O my God, I cry by day but you do not answer; and by night, but I find no rest" (v. 1, NRSV) But I did not blame God for your death— my anger was directed toward you. Persons often feel it is not "right" to be angry with someone who has died— but that anger is part of who we are; and it is important to offer our whole person to God if our whole person is to be healed. All of what your mom and I felt was expressed, poured out, offered for God's understanding and healing grace. And trust in God's grace becomes a source for a graceful attitude toward the one whose death has angered us (that's you, in this case, Pete!)

How can one explain the "turn" in the lament psalms, which Brueggemann and others have noticed?

It is surely more than a brainy chemical accident on a molecular level. Jesus doesn't explain it either. He simply says, "How fortunate are those who grieve. They shall be comforted." (Is it accurate to invert that saying, Peter? "How unfortunate are those who do not grieve. They cannot be comforted.")

Rather than an explanation of why the turn happens, I think we simply have the testimony from life experience concerning the importance of a decision. As Brueggemann observes, people of biblical faith decided long ago that loss, death, and grief are real and dangerous; but God can deal with them. Judging by what our life has been like in the last eight years, your mom and I had apparently already made that faith decision before Tim called with the very, very, very bad news.

As promised, we have been comforted. And most of the time, as epitomized in one lovely evening in south Italy, life for you mom and me is, indeed, sweet.

Love, Dad

Life Choosing Life

January 14, 2007

Dear Peter,

I want to say more about why I think you may be getting these letters. My belief is connected with my claim that we live in a universe that is essentially alive and relational, and that human life is the epitome of the relational universe in which we live.

Maybe the reason that Jesus had such a powerful effect on people is because he was more Personal than anyone else has ever been.

For me the continuing transformational effect of personal relationships in the early Christian communities is the evidence for belief in the resurrection of Jesus. And I see no reason why I should not believe that the personal, life-giving love embodied in Jesus should not continue for any of us after death.

That is why I am writing these letters to you, Peter.

For me, not to believe in life after death is an intellectually respectable choice.

To believe in life after death is also an intellectually respectable choice. Either choice is an inference grounded in the evidence of one's own observations and experience. Certainly, it is a leap of faith to jump from a belief in a relational universe to a belief in life after death. But it is a leap from what for me is a solid ground of personal experience.

My choice to believe in resurrection is not simply a product of my somewhat expansive view of theology and science. The faith in resurrection that has pulled your mom and me though the slough of grief is grounded in our own previous life experience. I am not speaking now of some "near-death experience." I do not doubt those testimonies, but such has not been mine. I am speaking of my own experience of near death of the spirit.

I do not know how much you know, Peter, about my own flirtations with self-imposed death. I have spoken of it with some others, especially in more recent years, but I do not remember talking about such times with you.

As you have seen in these letters, your grandmother and grandfather Mayer provided me early on with a fine basis for the development of my own faith. I do not remember ever doubting the love of God, and as far as I can remember, I always believed that love included everybody, including people who did some pretty bad things. But there were some rather severe flaws in my parents' relationship with each other, and in their parenting of my brother David and me—flaws which left me with very serious doubts about the value of my self. I struggled with low self-esteem throughout my childhood and for years afterward.

Of course it didn't help that I really was a different kind of kid. Growing up in Ohio farmland, my peers went barefoot, wore bib overalls, and did important things like slopping hogs, spreading manure, and driving a team. I wore sandals and short pants, read books, and sang boy-soprano solos. (There were some compensations; for a couple of years the parsonage had the only indoor toilet for miles around!)

I once made a bid to "get in" by joining 4-H. I wanted to raise a calf to compete in the county fair. Your necessarily frugal grandparents proposed instead a vegetable garden. One evening the 4-H met at our neighbor-boy's farm, a guy a year older than me with whom I had a love/hate relationship. When he saw me walking toward his place, he pulled one of the other 4-H-ers aside, saying "C'mere, I want to tell you something funny about 'ol Mayer."

I turned around and went home, not feeling well, I explained to your grandparents, accepting their invitation to join them in a glass of Kool-Aid by our badminton court. Thus the vegetable garden languished. And so did I much of the time up through high school, although I tried to hide it under the cover of music and theatre and funny stories for the school paper.

I fully expected that all would be better when I got into Elmhurst College, the church-related school I'd heard about all my life. But I soon discovered that at college I was still the same person I'd always been, feeling that I was failing in friendships just like always. After about only eight or ten weeks, I simply ran, taking a train as far west as my cash on hand would carry me. The police in Dubuque picked me up after the custodian of the Methodist church found me sleeping on a pew pad.

Finding a bottle of pills in my pocket, an officer asked, "You got headaches?"

"My only headache is myself, I guess," I answered.

After a night in jail, your very frightened grandparents arrived. I'll never forget the look of bewildered concern on the face of my dad when he came through the door of my cell.

"Hi Don."

I don't remember what I had expected from your grandparents, but there was something in my dad's look and tone which caused me to think that perhaps I had always misunderstood how my father regarded me. In that moment the seed of a new life was planted. That seed bore abundant fruit, Pete, but only after a very long time, with a lot of painful personal struggle.

Released from jail with no charge, not knowing what else to do, your grandparents took me back to Elmhurst. The college president, not knowing what else to do, invited me to dinner at his home. Then not knowing what else to do, he sent me to a local physician who

154

had served in WW2 and presumably knew something about young men with personal problems.

"Are you a pre-the?" (a pre-theological student).

"Well, technically, yes."

"You've probably been doing a lot of praying."

"Yes, I have."

"Well, you'd better stop that for a while . . ."

I don't remember what else he may have said. By that time I had decided he wasn't really interested in me either.

After a couple of days back in the dorm, I swallowed thirty-six headache pills, got very sick, threw up, and landed in the college infirmary. Your grandfather came to take me home. It was a long silent night-time train ride.

It wasn't long before I was considering various more effective ways of ending my life. Fortunately, one Sunday after church (I always hit bottom after church) I managed to admit to my distressed parents how bad I was feeling. Not knowing what else to do, they called our long-time family physician, Dr. Z.

He came to our home immediately and asked to talk with me privately. I tried to explain how badly I felt about myself. To Dr. Z, my story was incredulous. He only knew me as an honor student, a popular class leader, the star master of ceremonies at the Senior Class night.

"Why?" he asked.

"I think it has something to be with my being a p.k."

"A what?"

"A preacher's kid."

Not knowing what else to do, he gently asked me to come to his office the following day. I did. He gave me a diagnosis in case the Selective Service Board wondered what I was doing at home: "nervous exhaustion." He gave me the first of a series of vitamin B shots. Then he

instructed me to go see his friend J. who owned and op-
erated the sawmill five miles north of town.

"It will do you good to do some outside work for a
change."

I went. At that point I did not look like the Paul
Bunyan type. I weighed 118 pounds. It took another
intervention from Dr. Z before Mr. J risked the hire.
So I spent that long, frigid winter piling lumber in the
sawmill in Deerbrook, Wisconsin—the most important
winter in my life.

Dr. Z was right. I did feel a lot better about me,
at least half the time—my spirit would rise with the
Thursday pay check and drop on Sunday afternoon. I
had never been physically strong. I gained thirty-five
pounds in two months, all muscle. Photos show me
so suntanned that everybody else in the picture looks
anemic.

I snuck around the no-trespassing-in-prayer-
property sign by limiting myself to the Lord's Prayer. I
noticed for the first time that Jesus said we should pray
in the first person plural—very useful for assisting my
relationships with my fellow sawmill workers, all of
whom wondered what the hell a guy like me was doing
in a place like that! Above all, I had long hours to think
about how it was that I thought about myself the way I
did—and began the long process of thinking about myself differently.

I returned to Elmhurst in fall and sailed though,
four years of memories I cherish.

In my senior year, as you have heard me recount
numerous times, I was appointed to the Freshman Week
Committee who welcomed the incoming students a
week before everybody else came to the campus—a
viewpoint with a considerable advantage one might say,
right, Pete? And as you know your mom was among
those to be welcomed.

I later learned that she had come to EC by means of what can only be described as hard work and heroic determination. The dysfunction in my family was hidden. The dysfunction in your mom's family could hardly have been more blatant. Mom Lester, as we called her (the name from her second marriage), married your grandfather Almquist in order to get away from her own domineering mother. The newlyweds were separated some months before your mom was born and your mom and baby Lynnea went to that domineering mother.

Your mom landed in the first foster home when domineering mother kicked them both out of her house. You mom was told by family friends that the first foster family was 'bad'. No explanation of why that term fit.

The second foster family was marvelously loving and certainly the source of the buoyant hope which characterizes your mom, even when she sees little reason for hope. She stayed with the Sayles family from age two to six. (She kept in touch with Mom Sayles all her life). When the Sayles family began to express an interest in adopting little 'Nea', Mom Lester yanked her out and placed her in the Hillside Children's Home, where she stayed in a dormitory room for seven years.

During those years, Mom Lester provided mostly elegant dreams and heartbreaking disappointments, aggravated by her addiction to scotch.

Your grandpa Almquist fortunately blessed your mom with his genuinely caring presence every other weekend. The professional photo of the two of them together shows the cutest and for those moments at least the happiest kindergartner I've ever seen.

Somehow in those years, your mom developed a smile that lights the room and an ability to make every person she meets feel like she thinks they are the most important persons in the universe.

Your grandfather Almquist's remarriage rescued your mom from the children's home—against the advice of his pastor who said, "Better you should leave the girl in the home; she'll only be trouble for you." They chose another church for the wedding.

So for the first time in her life, at age 14 your mom lived with part of her family. She had a room of her own. But before long, she was asked to pay a little rent out of her earnings from an after school job.

Her parents did not actually divorce until your mom was eight. Each wanted her to testify against the other. In their entire lifetime, they never stopped blaming each other. And of course, each had no doubt that any financial support was the other's responsibility. And in the Almquist household any possible financial support for a college education was pre-committed to the newborn son, your uncle Karl.

Nevertheless, your mom scraped together enough earnings to get into Elmhurst College where she continued working day and night to pay her way—and even to earn train fare to visit your Almquist grandparents at Christmas time.

It is no surprise to you, Pete, to learn that after the Freshman Week scouting, I kept a very hopeful eye on this gorgeous freshman: "Lynnea"—what a lovely name!—from Rochester, New York, where she lived on Stone Road—even her address was glamorous!

I helped plan the mid-semester Student Christian Association Retreat at George Williams College Camp, Lake Geneva, Wisconsin. I was thrilled to discover that Lynnea had registered for the weekend. It was snowing heavily when we arrived. I owned the only pair of skis at college. We had snowball fights up by the Yerkes observatory. The weather cleared for incredibly beautiful moonlight on deep fresh snow. I proposed a walk. She said yes. We walked and talked. I proposed an early morning walk on the frozen lake. She said yes.

I was filled with astonished joy that a woman of such dazzling charm, with whom all the guys on campus were in love, was apparently actually quite interested in me. Unbelievable, Pete. After fifty years, it still is!

One certain thing we each brought from our respective family of origin experience was a tremendous calling to a kind of marriage and family life different from what either of us had experienced growing up. And for the most part, we succeeded. We cherish the memories of nearly every one of those fifty-plus years, filled with great adventures in family life and love. But we were also plagued with the negative left-overs from those childhood years. We smiled as we said when we celebrated our fiftieth anniversary, "Forty-eight of the best years of our life!"

Of course, we were not so different from most other couples. In a sermon, our Plymouth preacher Tony quoted a report indicating that 85 percent of American families were dysfunctional. "Actually," Tony said with a grin, "most of us clergy think that estimate is a too low!"

But marriage was more difficult than we could ever have imagined. We did our first counseling while still in seminary, shortly after Tim was born. It helped. A lot.

The low point came, as you know Peter, some thirty years later, when I actually left your mom for a short while, thinking that I was in love with somebody else. It was a terrible time. Your mom, she faced the abandonment she never dreamed she would face again. As for me, I came to feel that I had finally messed up my life after all. I remember one skeletal gray day when it occurred to me that suicide was not necessary since I was already as good as dead anyway.

You three kids hung in there with us, somehow an enormous help, gracefully not taking sides, caring for both of us.

Weeks of counseling followed for both your mom and I. But ultimately I was saved by a faint trust in the remote possibility that there might still be more to my life and our marriage than what I had come to believe. So also, I was saved by trust in the grace of God, mediated by a few close friends, and you three, and above all by your mom.

We began again with the move out here, to be closer to you three. And our life since then? Look to the last line from the text that I often used for a marriage service: "You have kept the best wine for now!" (John 2:12, New English Bible)!

So what I am saying, Peter, is that the belief in resurrection that your mom and I share is simply the extension of the evidence of personal resurrection in our own experience. I speak from that experience when I say in a funeral sermon that: "God's comfort comes though our trust that just as God raised Jesus from the dead, so we trust that God raises the one we grieve to God's loving presence—and in time raises us from the depth of grief to life which has the goodness which God intends for us."

Now Peter, let me propose another dimension of this resurrection phenomenon. (I hope you are not bored! If indeed you are getting these letters, you know more about this stuff than I do).

Remember when you three were little and mom took the three of you down to Florida for a visit with her mom? Mom had never broken the relationship with Mom Lester. (Mom Lester and *her* mother did not speak with each other for the last 29 years of your Grandma Bergman's life!) But up to that point in our marriage, your mom had never risked a visit with Mom Lester without me around. Now your mom made a deliberate choice to relate to her own mother face to face, with honesty, grace, and forgiveness. I will never forget the way Lynnea looked when she got off the plane when you four came back. You all looked Florida sun-kissed—but she was absolutely radiant!

Your mom's act of forgiveness was an act of liberation—for your mom. No longer was her life to be dominated by her mother's abandonment. It was a new life for Mom Lester too. It cleared away some of the smog of guilt—although addiction to scotch and deeply ingrained mental habits limited her newness of life.

See what I'm getting at, Pete? In the act of forgiveness the forgiver gets a new life. The forgiven one is offered a new life as well—but since the forgiver does not control acceptance, to forgive is to at least act for one's own well-being, one's own release into new life.

With no forgiveness there can be no movement. So Jesus says to the paralyzed man, "Your sins are forgiven—pick up your pad and get moving." (Mark 2). Forgiveness is essential for life giving, at the very least a survival tactic. For human life at least, forgiveness is as essential as oxygen.

To participate in the act of forgiveness either as giver or receiver is to participate in God's ability to make all things new, that is, to participate in the power of the resurrection.

So the struggle for both your mom and myself to overcome the wounds of early childhood by learning to trust in forgiveness and grace, resulted in a resilient hope in the midst of our deepest grief. In all, we were already participating in God's gift of new life.

Now Peter, here is one more really weird thing. Your mom and I have always shared a love of music. It was part of our courtship. I was business manager for the college choir; naturally she became my secretary! And on that warm, August night under the little tree in our friend Ray's back yard in Buffalo when I asked your mom to marry me, and she said yes, we could hear through Ray's bedroom window a lovely recording of the Brahms *Requiem*.

"They that sow in tears shall reap in joy . . ."

"The redeemed of the Lord shall come rejoicing . . . and tears and sighing shall flee from them . . . and joy everlasting shall be their portion. . ."

At this moment, Peter, I cannot express my goosebump awe at the long arc of coincidence. And the mysteriously powerful truth in Jesus' observation: "How fortunate those who grieve! They shall receive comfort!"

Fortunate indeed—from lament to sweetness!
Thanks be to God!
Love, Dad

P.S. See you later, Pete!

A Final Letter to Peter

10 p.m., Nov. 1, 2009

Dear Peter,
At last, mom and I got to sing the Brahms *Requiem* with Plymouth choir, 65 voices, 23-piece orchestra—wonderful! Standing ovation, went on and on, performers and audience all joining in the applause, ultimately for Brahms and God, I think! Then mom and I found each other, hugged and sobbed about you, more in joy than pain. I wore your black dress shoes.

See you, Pete!
Love, Dad

Epilogue

On Fathers Filled with Sadness and Joy

WALTER BRUEGGEMANN

I have known Don and Lynnea Mayer for over fifty years
... classmates, neighbors, friends, colleagues in ministry. Together "through many toils and snares we have
already come." I had known Peter as a young lad, but
not as an adult. As a father of two sons, however, I know
enough to want to respond to Don's collection of deeply
moving letters to Peter.

As is my wont (and most often my task), such a
moving articulation pushes me to biblical texts, to ask
about fathers and sons in Scripture who anticipate the
transactions between Don and Peter. When I ponder
fathers-and-sons, I am led to two texts in Scripture,
though many others might be considered.

I

In Genesis 27 we are offered quite a long and full narrative account of the flawed nature of Abraham's family.
Father Isaac (son of Abraham) is about to give his blessing to his firstborn son Esau. Through sly planning and
careful manipulation abetted by his mother, Rebecca,
Jacob (a second son) deceived his aged, blind father and
secured the family blessing that properly belonged to his
older brother. Isaac, being deceived, smelled his son and
kissed his son, and then he blessed Jacob (vv.22–29).

"As soon as Isaac had finished blessing Jacob" (the dishonest son), Esau came to receive his father's blessing that was rightly his (v. 30). When Esau asked his father for a blessing, in that instant Isaac figured out the deception, how he had been duped by his second son. He knew immediately that things had gone awry and that his family order was disrupted. The narrative says, "Isaac trembled violently" (v. 33). Isaac's entire world was shattered! And his son Esau, when he realized his loss to his brother, "he cried out with an exceedingly great and bitter cry, and said to his father, 'Bless me, me also, father'" (v. 34)! Then he asked his father: "'Have you not reserved a blessing for me'" (v. 36)? "'Bless me, me also, father!' And Esau lifted up his voice and wept" (v. 38).

The narrative, of course, is remote from Don and Peter. Except it voices all of the pathos-filled dimensions of father-son transactions. There is, in such transaction, always flaw, failure, and deception. And the outcome of such flaw, failure, and deception is "violent trembling" by the father and "bitter weeping" by the son. The father trembles and the son weeps; both are helpless, both carried away a fatedness thy cannot resist. The other son, Jacob, lurks at the edge of the scene. He must have observed father and son huddled together in their helplessness, saddened beyond speech, immobilized by loss, ready for solace, but finding very little.

The story is remote from Don and Peter, because there is no deception in the Don-Peter case. There is, to be sure, "stupidity" (Don's word) about a seatbelt, but it does not matter about deception or stupidity. What matters is brokenness, weakness, wistfulness, helplessness, sadness . . . and the need to go on living.

We do not learn much from the ongoing narrative about either son Esau or father Isaac. We know that Esau continued to be deceived by his brother Jacob (Gen 33:15–17). But the end of the story of the father is reported in Genesis 35:27–29. It turns out, so the narrative goes, that Isaac lived a full life: "Now the days of Isaac were one hundred eighty years" (Gen 35:28).

More than that, his final scene presents the two brothers reconciled enough to be together at his grave: "And Isaac breathed his last; he died and was gathered to his people, old and full of days; and his sons Esau and Jacob buried him" (Gen 35:29).

We know something about that reconciliation from the meeting in chapter 33. However it happened, that reconciliation must have pleased the old father to notice that his family had been repaired, not without scars, but repaired. The father who had "trembled violently" at the fracture of the family, died content.

Isaac, in the memory of Israel, is a lesser figure sandwiched between his greater father Abraham and his greater son Jacob. He is, however, remembered on his own terms. When the church, in Hebrews 11, was ready to recite the names of the great persons of faith, Isaac received and honorable mention: "By faith Isaac invoked blessing for the future on Jacob and Esau" (Heb 11:20).

In that memory Isaac blessed both sons and thereby created twin futures. The memory does not find it necessary to retell the entire tale of trembling and weeping and deception and alienation. All of that is for the moment forgotten; it can, however, be kept in storage while other matters are celebrated. It is like that for Don in the end. Nothing about Peter is forgotten, nothing of the sadness or the loss or the treasure that he is. But by the end of the correspondence with Peter, Don, not unlike father Isaac, has arrived at a new well-being . . . even joy. We do not know how that father Isaac found joy, but we dare imagine that his faith ("by faith") permitted his beginning again, even with the continuing power of enduring scars. It was "for the joy that was set before him" that he went on with his life, post-fracture (Heb 12:2).

II

The second father-son narrative in the Bible that strikes me as poignant in this context is that of father David and son Absalom. In fact, David's family is in disarray. Absalom, a son "much praised" and "without blemish" (2 Sam 14:25), first appears in the family narrative when he steps forward to avenge his sister, Tamar, who has been violated by another brother. David, the father who cannot manage his family, takes affront at Absalom's violent act of the elimination of his brother Amnon. We are told that at Amnon's death, "David mourned for his son day after day" (2 Sam 13:37), perhaps more so because it was an act of family violence.

But such grief, as Don has discovered, has its limit as an occupying force. We are told that after three years of grief, David turned his attention to his son whom he had rejected, Absalom: "And the heart of the king went out, yearning for Absalom; for he was now consoled over the death of Amnon" (2 Sam 13:39).

David, a complex man, is grieved, but then filled with yearning. He runs the emotional gamut of a father, as fathers must do with sons, as Don has done with Peter. Absalom's restoration to David's presence, nonetheless, is not easy, and must be carefully choreographed. Finally, after much careful scheming, the son is back in the presence of his royal father: "Then Joab went to the king and told him; and he summoned Absalom. So he came to the king and prostrated himself with his face to ground before the king; and the king kissed Absalom" (2 Sam 14:33). The son bowed deeply before the father. The father kissed the son. All is well, even after the murder, so great is the yearning of the father for the son.

Except that Absalom could not leave it there. He seeks to usurp his father's royal function, and because of his style, his glamour, and his attentiveness, he "stole

the hearts of the people of Israel (2 Sam 15:6). Thus
the stage is set for competition between father and son.
David is ferocious in defense of his throne, and will not
be cheated out of it, even by his son. The confrontation
of father and son is public and military and violent.
There is nothing fatherly about David in his hot, violent
pursuit of Absalom the rebel.

Until Absalom is killed! The son is killed as a rebel
by David's most loyal men (2 Sam 18:14–15). They are
proud of the death of the rebel and report the end of the
challenge to David's rule: "Then the Cushite came; and
the Cushite said, "Good tidings for my lord the king!
For the Lord has vindicated you this day, delivering you
from the power of all who rose up against you" (2 Sam
18:31). But the king inquires of Absalom, for he cares
more about the son than he does about the war: "The
king said to the Cushite, 'Is it well with the young man
Absalom'" (2 Sam 18:32a)? The news bearer, however,
still does not get it, thinking of Absalom as a rebel and
not as a son: "The Cushite answered, "May the enemies
of my lord the king, and all who rise up to do you harm,
be like that young man" (2 Sam 18:32b).

The news carrier had neglected to notice that the
rebel is also a son. And indeed he could easily have forgotten it, because until this moment in the narrative,
David never once refers to Absalom as his "son." Not
until his death!

At his death, Absalom is no longer taken by David
to be a threat or a challenge or a rebel. Now, for the first
time, Absalom is "son." Father David looks away from
his military maps and disregards his military advisors.
At the moment of the death report he is consumed with
his painful fatherliness:

"The king was deeply moved, and went up to the
chamber over the gate, and wept; and as he went, he
said, 'O my son Absalom, my son, my son Absalom!
Would I have died instead of you, O Absalom, my son,

my son'" (2 Sam 18:33)! It is reported that the king was
"deeply moved"; well, in fact he quivered in agitation . . .
not unlike father Isaac before him. He wept! He wept the
way a father will weep at the death of a son. He wept and
called out the name of his son . . . twice. Five times in
this moment he calls him "my son." It is like a flood after
alienation, all the yearning kinship that the father has re-
pressed while he played king. Now he abandons all that
is regal and accepts his father role that is one of limitless,
bitter, sobbing grief without comfort. He knows that he
is old and son Absalom was young, and he would have
taken his place in death. Only, he cannot! And because
he cannot, he must dissolve in grief, partly loss, partly
awareness of his long-term failure, partly grief that can
be cried but scarcely voiced.

Joab, David's hatchet man, wants the father to
quit his *fatherness* and return to his *kingliness* (2 Sam
19:1–3). But David is not finished with his fatherly task,
as a father never is. In defiance of the demands of Joab,
David is moved again into the depths of his fatherly
loss: "The king covered his face, and the king cried with
a loud voice, 'O my son Absalom, O Absalom, my son,
my son'" (2 Sam 19:4)! Two times he names again, three
times he calls him "my son." The rhetoric is so repeti-
tious, because there is nothing else to say . . . only the
name, only the connection, the connection, and then the
name:

"The king covered his face, and the king cried with
a loud voice, 'O my son Absalom, O Absalom, my son,
my son'" (2 Sam 19:4)! Eventually the king, at the behest
of Joab, puts on his regal manner and does his royal duty
(2 Sam 19:8). But he is not finished with his son and will
not be finished with his son for a very long, painful time.
It does not matter that his son was a killer and a traitor
and a rebel. None of that matters. What matters is the
palpable, bodily link that has endured beyond all formal
connections; and that palpable, bodily link ends in grief.

It ends in grief without end because David will not finish being a father.

We are able to get from the scene of grief in 2 Samuel 18:19 to the lyric of 2 Samuel 22 only by a complex editorial process. If, however, we take the text as we have it, we find David now in a new place of confidence and buoyancy. We do not know how he got from a place of grief to this celebrative lyric, any more than Don can tell us fully how his life became "sweet" again. What is clear is that David lingered long over the death of the son, but he did not linger there finally. Finally he sings of faith just as Don ends his correspondence pondering the proof of Easter. In a lyrical retrospective that anticipates the resolved faith of Don, David affirms of God:

> He said:
> The LORD is my rock, my fortress, and my deliverer,
>> my God, my rock, in whom I take refuge,
> my shield and the horn of my salvation,
>> my stronghold and my refuge
>> my savior; you save me from violence,
> I call upon the LORD, who is worthy to be praised,
>> and I am saved from my enemies. (2 Sam 22:2–4)

The next verse lacks specificity. We are, nevertheless, free to connect the verses to the death of Absalom. David speaks exactly of death in the same way that Don can tell Peter of his skirmish with death and perdition and Sheol:

> For the waves of *death* encompassed me,
>> the torrents of *perdition* assailed me;
> the cords of *Sheol* entangled me,
>> the snares of *death* confronted me. (2 Sam 22:5–6)

Such a father in faith knows that in such a snare, the proper turn is to the God of life:

Epilogue

In my distress I called upon the Lord;
>   to my God I called.
From his temple he heard my voice,
>   and my cry came to his ears. (2 Sam. 22:7)

David did not know how the divine hearing happens,
nor does Don know. Only the ones who have been heard
can attest that after an unbearable death there is still
possible a fatherly joy. And so David, in his new season
of faith, can attest:

>   *By you* I can crush a troop,
>>   And *by my God* I can leap over a wall.
>   (2 Sam. 22:30)

I can leap over a wall! This is an act not to be committed
by a sad father but only by a father who has come to new
joy. He leaps over a barrier he thought he could never
clear; he knows perfectly well that he could not have
gotten there on his own. It is only "by you," by YHWH,
by the God of the gospel.

Thus David can come full circle. Before there was
any Absalom, David could boast: "David said, 'The
Lord, who saved me from the paw of the lion and from
the paw of the bear, will save me from the hand of the
Philistine.' So Saul said to David, 'Go, and may the Lord
be with you'" (1 Sam 17:37)! But then came Absalom
and the loss of such vigor. But when his grief was spent,
came again divine power to which Don can also attest. Peter's death drained everything out of his father,
but after loyal grief, Don, by the mercy of God—like
David—is again leaping over walls in joy.

III

The life of a father is inordinately complex, made complex by the reality of sons who draw close and move
away, who evidence devotion and who commit stupidity,

172

whose very being is a mix of joy and ache. I do not want to draw the narrative of Isaac and Jacob and Esau or the narrative of David and Absalom too close to the narrative of Don and Peter, for the differences are great. In the Don-Peter narrative, there was no deception that evoked violent trembling. In the Don-Peter narrative, there was no killing that caused alienation. But after those acute differences are noticed, we are permitted to appreciate the parallels between the narratives. The father-son relationship comes, inevitably I suspect, with the grief of loss and anguish and yearning. All of these fathers— Isaac, David, Don—know in deep ways that beyond father and son there is a third Easter player who is capable of "turning mourning into dancing" (Ps 30:11), capable of transposing tribulation into joy (John 16:33). That turn is a gift beyond explanation. It cannot be produced. It cannot even be anticipated. It can only be received in astonishment and gratitude when it is given.

I am very glad for this volume of letters and for Don's capacity for candid testimony through which he has "written himself" to wholeness. Don's testimony is an invitation to every father—including this one—about loss and possibility. His offer is a great gift to us all, a gift from Don, a gift from the Easter God who met Don and Lynnea in a cave and made all things new.

I write these lines toward Don and Lynnea with treasured memories, with awed gratitude, and with hope for fresh acres of newness. That newness surely continues to be the hope of Peter for his family and the hope of God, who abidingly holds Peter close.